Author:
Mary Ellen Sterling, M. Ed.

Illustrator:
Kathy Bruce

Cover Artist:
Blanca Apodaca La Bounty

Editors:
Karen J. Goldfluss, M.S. Ed.

Senior Editor:
Sharon Coan, M.S. Ed.

Art Direction:
Elayne Roberts

Product Manager:
Phil Garcia

Imaging:
Alfred Lau

Publishers:
Rachelle Cracchiolo, M.S. Ed.
Mary Dupuy Smith, M.S. Ed.

FOCUS ON ARTISTS

Teacher Created Materials, Inc.
P.O. Box 1040
Huntington Beach, CA 92647
©1994 Teacher Created Materials, Inc.
Made in U.S.A.

ISBN-1-55734-494-9

Table of Contents

Introduction

Art is a form of self-expression that has progressed and undergone change throughout the stages of human development. What began as a means of communicating by scratching out pictures on a cave wall has evolved into a complex system of design elements. Artists are no longer limited to chalk and slate for their tools; today there are any number of materials available to artists. These new raw materials have spawned whole movements in the art world and their influence is felt even today.

Not everyone appreciates a great piece of art nor does everyone agree on what constitutes "good" art. Our cultural differences generally condition us as to what is beautiful or pleasing to our eye. However, ideas about art can be changed and enlarged to encompass a broader spectrum of works. Young people can be taught how to judge an art piece according to a set of criteria. That does not mean they have to like a particular work but at least they will be armed with the proper tools necessary to understand and appreciate an art form for what it is—an artist's expression of his or her inner self.

It is the purpose and intent of *Focus on Artists* to acquaint students with famous and not-so-famous artists and their styles. This will be accomplished through a biography of each artist followed by an art lesson which will help students explore some of the elements employed by that particular artist. Extension activities allow for further exploration of each artist.

A secondary purpose of this book is to enhance the students' knowledge of art in history. To accomplish this end, artists have been grouped according to three distinct historical periods—Renaissance and Baroque, the Nineteenth Century, and the Twentieth Century—so that the changes in artistic formats can be seen in a continual time line.

This resource contains basic information on thirty-three different artists through the ages. Hopefully, the inspiring stories of these men and women and the accompanying activities will motivate students to explore the world of art on their own.

Using the Pages

How you use the pages in this book depends on any number of factors which may include school or district guidelines, learning levels of the students, personal teaching styles and goals, and how well the study of the artist fits a particular theme.

The following descriptions of the book's features are intended to help you get the most from each page.

Sections

The artists presented in this book are categorized by the time period in which they lived. The book is divided into three time periods: Renaissance and Baroque Artists, Nineteenth Century Artists, and Twentieth Century Artists.

Biographies

Each artist is introduced with a biographical account of his or her life and accomplishments. These biographies can be read aloud to students, copied for group or individual student use, or used as a teacher resource.

You may wish to create a book of biographies for class use. Copy each biography, punch holes along one side of the papers, and assemble them into a three-ring binder. Add dividers labeled Renaissance and Baroque Artists, Nineteenth Century Artists, and Twentieth Century Artists. Write and add biographies of any other artists that you study.

Themes

To focus on a particular theme, such as Women Artists of the Twentieth Century, refer to the lists on pages 8, 36, and 65. Write each artist's name on a separate index card and place the cards in a paper bag. Have each students or pair of students draw a name. Provide them with a choice of activities to complete. Students can share what they have learned with the whole class or in small groups.

Activities

Extension activities follow each biography. They are provided so that you may vary the way lessons are presented. Choose those which best suit your classroom needs and adapt them to fit your students' abilities and your teaching style. Another option is to allow students to choose their activities.

Activity pages are written to accommodate a number of learning styles. Determine which of these activities may be suitable for your students. Adapt activities to meet your teaching style and students' needs and abilities.

A list of recommended reading completes the activity page. In addition to these selected reading materials, check your school, public, or university library for other titles.

Art Resources

Both you and your students are anxious to learn about different artists. You cannot wait to try the various art techniques. Only one thing is lacking — an art reproduction related to a particular lesson. Even if you do not live close to a large museum and you do not have an unlimited budget, it is possible to have art in your classroom. Check out the surprising sources listed below.

✔ Calendars

Many wall and mini-calendars provide you with a year's worth of different pictures by an artist (Matisse, Monet, O'Keefe, etc.). Check out gift shops, book stores, card shops, and stationery stores for available titles. Purchase these after the first of the year when prices are reduced.

✔ Reader's Digest

Collect all the old issues of *Reader's Digest* that you can because the back covers feature a different art work every month. Enlist parents and your colleagues to help you with your collection.

✔ Professional Magazines

Read professional journals such as *Teaching, Creative Classroom,* and *Instructor.* Often they contain art-related articles and even pull-out posters that can be displayed in your classroom.

✔ Book Stores

Many book stores offer a bargain table of items at reduced prices. Look for books about individual artists, art history, or art techniques. Some book stores (and teacher supply stores) offer a number of community services such as classes, slide shows, and lectures about art for children and adults.

✔ Art Exhibits

Visit a local art gallery or invite a local artist to bring a portfolio of his or her work to your classroom. Check with the closest college or university for information about art displays and exhibits. Talk with someone in your city's art league for some possible sources of art works.

✔ Art Magazines

The local library may subscribe to a number of art magazines; preview them to see which ones are most appropriate for your use.

✔ Libraries

Besides art books, biographies of artists, art magazines, videos, and other art materials, libraries may display paintings. Art can sometimes be checked out for a time period similar to books. Ask your librarian if any of these materials are available. In addition to these materials, art classes and lectures may be offered through library extension groups.

Art Resources
(cont.)

On this page you will find more art resources at your disposal. In some cases you will have to write to companies to find out more about what they have to offer.

✔ Eyewitness Books

One of the most popular series to hit the children's book scene in recent years is *Eyewitness Books*. Each book in the series covers a different topic ranging from armor to flags to whales. The latest additions focus on art. Beautiful, full-color reproductions of art works are included in the pages and are accompanied by well-written text. Look for these and other titles in book stores, art supply stores, teachers' supply stores, and libraries.

✔ Williamson Publishing

EcoArt!, The Kids' Multicultural Art Book, and *Adventures in Art* and other Williamson books are available in book stores, but if not, you may want to order them on your own. While these texts do not contain reproductions of great art works, they do contain a number of arts and crafts experiences that can be used in conjunction with a particular artist you are studying. To receive a catalog write to:

Williamson Publishing Company
P.O. Box 185, Church Hill Road
Charlotte, Vermont 05445
802-425-2102 / 800-234-8791

✔ Mail-Order Catalogs

Before you throw away that unsolicited mail-order catalog, look through its pages to see if the company offers cards or stationery which feature the style of art you are studying. Often you can buy individual cards. They can be used as part of a card file "museum" that you build up. Laminate your purchases for extended use.

✔ Fine Arts Posters

Posters are a welcome addition to any classroom, especially when they reflect the theme of the current curriculum. Gift shops, art supply stores, record shops, large department stores, and even grocery stores may be a source for posters, but two outstanding sources are listed below; write to the addresses given for a catalog.

Metropolitan Museum of Art
Fifth Avenue at Adams Street
New York, New York 10028

Dale Seymour Publications
P.O. Box 10888
Palo Alto, California 94303
800-872-1100

(In addition to posters, Dale Seymour offers books about art, an art history time line, and a series of art prints for kindergarten through sixth grade.)

Larger than Life

Many of the artists featured in this book are literally larger than life. With their lively imaginations and their creative use of colors, line, and perspective, they bring excitement and vitality to everyday people, objects, and events. Other artists quietly bring their unique outlook to the art world, subtly changing the flavor of subsequent art works. Celebrate these individual differences with your students through any of the following activities.

1. Arrange students in pairs or small groups. Have them select a favorite painting and recreate the painting using costumes and props. Have each pair or group present themselves as a particular work to the rest of the class; they may have a narrator to explain the art piece and tell something about the artist.

    Note: The city of Laguna Beach, California, presents a Pageant of the Masters every summer during the months of July and August. You may want to contact the Laguna Beach Chamber of Commerce for information about this unusual and most dramatic display of live art. The address is:

    > Chamber of Commerce
    > 6357 Glenneyre
    > Laguna Beach, CA 92651

2. Have students dress as their favorite artist or in clothing representative of a specific time period (e.g., the Renaissance or the 1920s). If props and costumes are a problem, invite students to dress in the colors or patterns of a certain artist. For example, dress in blue tones to represent Picasso's blue period or wear polka dots to symbolize pointillism used by Seurat.

3. Create a wall chart of world events. For each artist highlighted, create an art sample and a brief summary of his or her artistic achievements and particular talents. Attach these samples to the classroom walls. Or, firmly attach a piece of rope across a wall and use clothespins or paper clips to hang the art samples and summaries. Above or below each entry, list on a large index card the years in which that artist lived and write a summary of some important world events that also took place in that same time period. By choosing artists from all three sections presented in this book, students should gain a thorough understanding of world events and be able to tie them together in a logical manner.

Art Terms

Listed below is a glossary of art terms that you may want your students to know. Use the terms for any of the following activities:

✦ Assign the words as a vocabulary and/or spelling list.

✦ Encourage students to employ the words in their daily vocabulary wherever possible.

✦ Cut and paste each word with its definition onto a separate index card; store the words alphabetically in an index card file. Add new words to the card file throughout the art lessons.

Abstract art: art which represents people, animals, and objects through simplified forms

Acrylic: synthetic resins used for painting

Avant-garde: a group of artists who initiate a new technique or style in defiance of the established art of the day

Collage: an art technique in which cut-up pieces of material are applied to a background to form one work of art

Foreshortening: a method in which objects are represented as if seen from an angle as opposed to a front view or a profile

Fine art: the collective name for all paintings, sculptures, drawings, and prints

Fresco: a mural or a wall painting

Impasto: oil paint that is applied very thickly

Medium: any material with which the artist works (e.g., watercolors, acrylics, oils, or chalks)

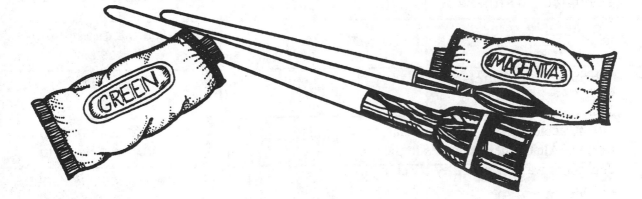

Mosaic: designs made by embedding small stones or glass in cement

Perspective: a technique used in painting to convey three dimensions on a flat surface

Pigment: a dry, powdered substance that is mixed with a suitable liquid to give color to paint

Renaissance: an era of cultural rebirth in Europe during the 15th and 16th centuries

Tempera: pigment mixed with an emulsion of egg yolk and water or egg and oil; used by early Renaissance painters

Water colors: pigments that have been mixed with water rather than oil

---

Renaissance and Baroque Artists

During the Middle Ages, art did not disappear, but certainly it was not a time when art flourished. Emphasis was on mosaics, frescoes, and stained glass windows which pictured saints and martyrs. With the beginning of the Renaissance came an awakening and a rebirth of lifelike art. A renewed interest and subsequent expansion in the sciences, along with the rediscovery of the Greco-Roman style, helped artists to make accurate visual images. Technical innovations and creative discoveries paved the way for more realistic styles.

The Middle Ages was a period in history during which the Catholic Church controlled the populace with a system known as feudalism. In this system people gave service to their king in return for land and protection. Toward the end of the fourteenth century, cities became powerful again and trade began to flourish. Universities emerged, bringing a rebirth of learning. It became an era of exploration which included the voyages of Columbus, Vasco da Gama, and Amerigo Vespucci.

This was the changing world for Leonardo da Vinci and other artists of his time. Major changes in art included the use of oil paints on canvas, the use of light and shadow, and the employment of pyramidical compositions in paintings.

In the 1600s, Baroque came onto the scene with its ornate and lavish style. It married the techniques of the Renaissance with the drama of Mannerism (at that time, art that featured distorted bodies). This movement began around 1600 and continued to be popular just until the nineteenth century.

Below is a listing of the artists represented in this section. Following each name and country of origin is a brief statement indicating particularly noteworthy achievements.

Artist	Country of Origin	Achievements
Sandro Botticelli (1444/45-1510)	Italy	*noted for his fantasy-like figures*
Rosalba Carriera (1675-1757)	Italy	*first artist to explore the uses of pastels*
Leonardo da Vinci (1452-1519)	Italy	*best known for the Mona Lisa, but was also a scientist and thinker*
Albrecht Dürer (1471-1528)	Germany	*first to use printmaking as a major art medium*
Thomas Gainsborough (1727-1788)	England	*known for his fashionable portraits*
Michelangelo (1475-1564)	Italy	*painter of the Sistine Chapel, sculptor and architect*
Rembrandt (1606-1669)	Holland	*best known for his realistic portraits*
Diego Velázquez (1599-1660)	Spain	*considered to be Spain's major gift to the art world*
Elisabeth Vigee-Lebrun (1755-1842)	France	*known as one of the best portrait painters of her time*

Sandro Botticelli

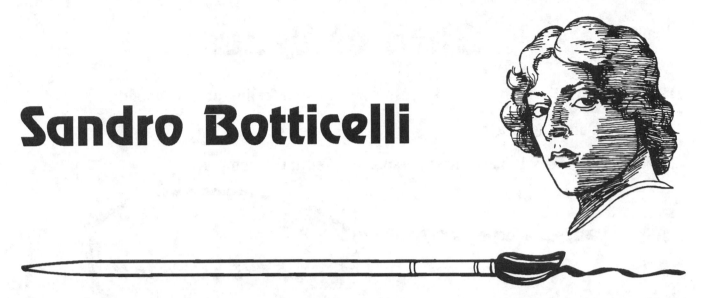

During the early Renaissance, painters such as Leonardo da Vinci and Michelangelo had begun to depict their subjects as solid, lifelike figures. They studied human anatomy so that they could make their subjects look as real as possible. Perspective was introduced into paintings, giving objects a three-dimensional appearance. Sandro Botticelli's paintings defied this new convention. Botticelli's flat, not-so-realistic looking figures made him one of the favorite artists of the time.

Sandro Botticelli was born in either 1444 or 1445 in Florence, Italy. Born Alessandro di Mariano Filipepi, he changed his name when he went to live with his older brother who was nicknamed "Botticello" (which meant "little barrel"). Botticello's job was pounding gold onto picture frames and some areas of artists' paintings (such as halos around people's heads). Young Sandro saw many works of art in his brother's workshop and probably met some of the artists themselves. By the age of 14, he was sent to work with one of the greatest master painters in Florence — Filippo Lippi. While in Lippi's charge, Sandro learned basic art techniques of mixing colors, cleaning brushes, and preparing walls for painting. He was taught how to draw and paint by Filippo Lippi himself.

At this time in history, it was common for wealthy patrons to pay an artist to work for them. Fortunately for Botticelli, the powerful Lorenzo de' Medici loved his paintings. The highly influential Medici saw to it that Botticelli was hired by his friends and family. Religious paintings were especially popular, and Botticelli painted for many churches in Florence as well as other cities in Italy. One of these paintings was so popular that copies were made without permission; artists today still have difficulty determining a fake from an original of this painting.

Perhaps Botticelli's most famous work is the Birth of Venus, a scene depicting the goddess of love standing on a sea shell. The figures depicting the winds appear to be floating in the air and all the forms have been outlined giving them a feeling of movement.

Botticelli, who lived to be 65 years old, remained popular until the end of his life when newer Renaissance artists stepped into the spotlight in which he had proudly stood.

Birth of Venus

Focus: Botticelli outlined his figures to give them a feeling of movement.

Activity: Outlining a face

Vocabulary: early Renaissance; perspective; outlining; tempera

Art Lesson

Materials

◆ old magazines

◆ scissors

◆ white paper, preferably card stock weight

◆ glue stick

◆ black thin-line marking pen

Directions

1. Have students examine a close-up of the face of Venus in Botticelli's *Birth of Venus.* Look for the outlines around her face and hair.

2. Direct students to find and cut out a portrait from the pages of a magazine.

3. Tell them to glue the picture to the white paper and allow it to dry.

4. With the black marker draw an outline around the head.

5. If possible, make copies of just the head of Venus (See *Renaissance Painters Coloring Book* by Andy Nelson, Culpepper Press, 1991, for a copy of this picture.). Give one to each student. Ask students to outline the faces and color in the details.

Extensions

1. Establish that Botticelli's birth name was Alessandro di Mariano Filipepi. Tell students to write a creative story explaining how Botticelli got his new name. Alternate activity: Ask students to tell what nickname they would choose for themselves.

2. Group students. Direct them to find examples of Botticelli's work and that of another Renaissance painter. Have students discuss how the two artists are similar and how they are different. Tell them to note the fantasy qualities that Botticelli gave to his people. Take an informal poll to find out who the students prefer — Botticelli or another Renaissance artist.

3. Michelangelo was another Renaissance artist whose patron was Lorenzo de' Medici. Possibly Michelangelo and Botticelli knew one another. Direct students to write a conversation the two artists might have had about one another's work.

4. Lorenzo de' Medici was called Lorenzo the Magnificent and virtually ruled Florence.

    ✦ Research this famous family and have students learn how one family influenced so many aspects of life in that great city.

    ✦ Have students tell who some of the other famous Medicis were and what they were noted for.

    ✦ Instruct students to write a story telling how Botticelli's life might have been different had he not been sponsored by Medici.

    ✦ Botticelli's *Adoration of the Magi* included a large number of members of the Medici family. Have students speculate on why Botticelli might do such a thing. For a real challenge the students can try to identify members of the family; the book, *Botticelli* by Mike Venezia (listed below) is an excellent resource for this activity.

Recommended Reading _____

Botticelli by Mike Venezia (Children's Press, Inc., 1991)

The Cambridge Introduction to Art: The Renaissance by Rosa Maria Letts (Cambridge University Press, 1991)

Great Painters by Piero Ventura (G.P. Putnam's Sons, 1984)

Renaissance Painters Coloring Book by Andy Nelson (Culpepper Press,1991)

Start Exploring Masterpieces by Mary Martin (Running Press, 1990) (This book includes 60 illustrations to color.)

Rosalba Carriera

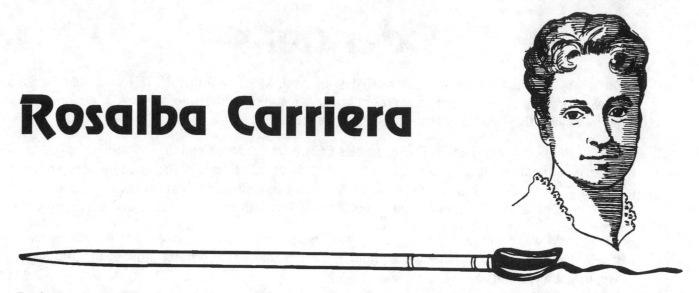

In the seventeenth century, it was very unusual for women to have a career outside of the home. They could paint and do various crafts, but that was in addition to their homemaking duties. Every once in a while a female would break the traditional stereotype of woman as wife, mother, and homemaker. Rosalba Carriera was one such woman.

Rosalba's artistic career began with the tiny oil paintings she created on small ivory boxes. When a family friend gave her a present of some lovely colored chalks, Rosalba quickly changed mediums. It is important to note that at this time soft chalks, also known as pastels, were a relatively new invention and were not widely used by artists. Carriera explored the unique properties of the chalks and learned how to build up layers of colors. By rubbing the chalk with her thumb she found that it was possible to create a lacy look. Her innovative uses of a relatively unknown medium gained her attention and popularity. Eventually her pastel portraits drew the attention of many members of royalty.

When a French art collector saw her work, he invited Rosalba to Paris. She and her family left their Venice home for France where Rosalba became the first artist to introduce pastel portraits there. Due to her efforts, pastel portraits became the vogue in Paris. As a result, she was invited to be a member of the French Academy of Painting; very few women then were so honored. In her homeland, she was inducted as a member of the Academy in Rome, Italy.

Known primarily for her portraits of others, Rosalba also painted some self-portraits. She is described as no great beauty and in a self-deprecating manner often portrayed herself as the tragic Muse with her brow encircled by a wreath of laurel. Tragically, her life ended on a sad note as she gradually lost her eyesight.

Pastel Painting

Focus: Pastels are an acceptable medium for portraits.

Activity: Creating a pastel portrait

Vocabulary: pastels; colored chalks; rococo

Art Lesson

Materials

- ✦ scrap paper
- ✦ colored chalks
- ✦ newspapers
- ✦ fixative or hair spray
- ✦ white drawing paper or construction paper

Directions

1. Encourage students to explore the different properties of chalk. On a piece of scrap paper, have them draw with the side of the chalk and then with the tip of the chalk. Note the differences. Tell them to rub the chalk along the paper and then rub it with one finger. Notice what happens to the color. Experiment with two or more colors.

2. Spread newspaper over the working surface to catch the chalk dust.

3. Tell students to choose a suitable subject for a portrait.

4. With the chalk, draw portraits on the paper.

5. When the pictures are completed, gently shake them over the newspaper. Spray with fixative or hair spray to seal the chalk.

Extensions

1. Explore the properties of chalk with this activity. Each participant will need a paintbrush, a small dish of water, a sheet of drawing paper, and some colored chalk.

    ✦ Dip the brush into the water and wet a small area of the paper.

    ✦ Immediately brush the chalk over the moistened area with one smooth stroke.

    ✦ Repeat the first and second steps until the picture is complete.

2. Research the roles of males and females during the seventeenth century. Discuss typical female duties and society's rules about what women could and could not do at that time. Compare these duties and rules to those of today.

3. Very few women were artists prior to the eighteenth century. Have students research any of the following early female painters.

    > ✦ Sofonisba Anguissola (1532-1625)
    > This Renaissance painter was from a wealthy Italian family who encouraged her and her five sisters to read, play musical instruments, write poetry, and paint.
    >
    > ✦ Lavinia Fontana (1552-1614)
    > Another Italian, she was the first woman artist to create paintings for large public places.
    >
    > ✦ Maria Sibylla Merian (1647-1717)
    > This German artist was known for scientific paintings and books about plants and insects.
    >
    > ✦ Rachel Ruysch (1664-1750)
    > Born in Holland, Rachel is considered to be one of the greatest still-life painters in that country.

4. The reigning style of the eighteenth century was rococo, a style which emphasized prettiness, delicacy, and a happy spirit. Have students find out more about rococo painting, interior decoration, and architecture. Tell them to design a living room complete with furniture in the rococo style.

Recommended Reading _____

History of Women Artists for Children by Vivian Sheldon Epstein (VSE Publisher, 1987)

17th and 18th Century Art by Ariane Ruskin (McGraw-Hill, 1969)

Leonardo da Vinci

As the world emerged from the Middle Ages, exploration, the sciences, and the arts began to flourish. The Renaissance became a time of rediscovery—an awakening. This was the changing world into which Leonardo da Vinci was born on April 15, 1452.

Leonardo's father was Ser Piero a secretary to the Signoria, or governing body, of the Florentine state. Because Ser Piero never married Leonardo's natural mother, Leonardo could not be accepted into any of the seven guilds (trade unions) nor could he attend the local university. He was, however, accepted as an apprentice in the workshop of artist Andrea del Verrocchio.

Under Andrea del Verocchio's tutelage, he learned about religious and classical subjects and was shown the proper methods of working with a variety of art mediums which included the traditional egg tempera painting and the techniques of the newly-introduced oil painting, sculpting wood and stone, modelling in clay, casting in bronze, silver, and gold, and making musical, navigational, and surgical instruments.

Although del Verrocchio kept Leonardo very busy in the workshop, da Vinci still found time to work on projects of his own. By the time he was twenty-six years old, da Vinci had completed his *Annunciation*. In preparation for this magnificent piece of work, he had drawn dozens of sketches. Some drawings included such details as the fold of draperies or the tilt of the head. Leonardo was to follow such intricate planning on all his subsequent art works.

After da Vinci had been under del Verrocchio's guidance in Florence for some eighteen years, he went to Milan as an ambassador. His duties as master of court festivities demanded that he design sets and costumes. Leonardo also designed new canals and modernized old ones and served as a court portrait painter. It was during this time in Milan that Leonardo completed *The Last Supper,* one of the most famous paintings ever created. (Around 1503 during a second stay in Milan, he painted the *Mona Lisa,* easily his most famous portrait.) He also worked on a full-scale model of the *Great Horse* as an equestrian monument to a member of the nobility. When the clay model was completed, it measured twenty-two feet (6.6 m) high without the rider. During his remaining years, da Vinci studied the sciences, particularly flight and the body. He identified hardening of the arteries as a cause of death and studied the aging process. His findings were recorded in books of drawings and notes and were studied in Italian medical schools for years. At the age of sixty-seven, Leonardo died peacefully, leaving behind a legacy that still remains.

The Last Supper

Focus: Leonardo da Vinci's portraits embody the Renaissance discoveries of perspective, anatomy, and composition.

Activity: Drawing an egg tempera portrait

Vocabulary: Renaissance; egg tempera; fresco; casting

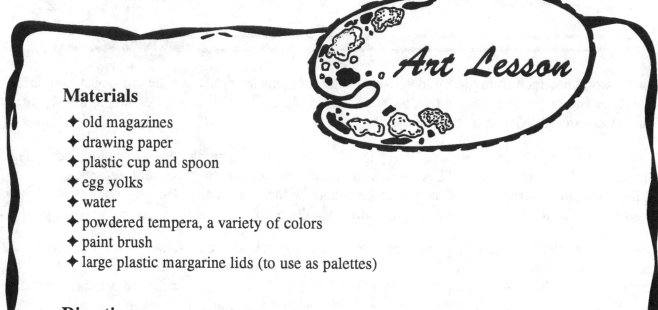

Materials

- ✦ old magazines
- ✦ drawing paper
- ✦ plastic cup and spoon
- ✦ egg yolks
- ✦ water
- ✦ powdered tempera, a variety of colors
- ✦ paint brush
- ✦ large plastic margarine lids (to use as palettes)

Directions

1. Ask students to observe the painting of *The Last Supper*. With the students, discuss the perspective from which da Vinci painted this scene. Notice the movement of the figures and how they are grouped. Establish that Leonardo was experimenting with an oil/tempera emulsion which he applied to a plaster wall. The results were disastrous, and today it is being restored inch by inch.

2. Students will use an egg tempera which is a medium that da Vinci frequently employed. Prepare your own egg tempera using the following recipe.

    In the cup break up the egg yolks and add half as much water; for example, if there are 2 tablespoons (30 mL) of yolk, add 1 tablespoon (15 mL) of water.

    On the lid, combine a small amount of the yolk/water mix with a bit of powdered tempera. Mix thoroughly.

    Continue combining the yolk/water mixture with a powdered tempera until all colors desired have been mixed.

3. Group students. Direct each group to draw a picture using egg tempera paints.

Extensions

1. According to the author of *The Annotated Mona Lisa* (see listing below), the definition of a *Renaissance man* is "...an omnitalented individual who radiates wisdom." Have students explain why Leonardo da Vinci was a good example of a Renaissance man.

2. While Leonardo was in Milan, he built a 22-foot (6.6 m) clay model of the duke's horse. Ultimately, it was to have been cast in bronze but war broke out and the bronze had to be used for weapons. Assign a group of students to find out who was involved in the war, the war's causes, and what became of the huge statue. Have them present their findings to the rest of the class.

3. Although da Vinci could write and draw with either hand, he preferred to use his left hand. Wherever he went he had a notebook in his pocket and kept sketches and notes about people, buildings, animals, plants, and designs. All of the writing was done in mirror writing which read from right to left. Give students an opportunity to simulate Leonardo's genius with either of these two activities.

   ✦ Instruct students to carry a small notebook with them at all times for a period of five school days. Each day they are to draw or sketch people, buildings, vehicles, designs, or any other interesting things they see. At the end of the week, they are to exchange the notebooks with a partner or share them in small groups.

   ✦ Each participant will need a small mirror for this project. Write a sentence about da Vinci on the chalkboard and tell students to copy it on a sheet of paper. Hold the mirror up to the writing to get an idea of what mirror writing looks like. Challenge students to print the sentence using mirror writing so that when it is held up to a mirror the writing looks normal.

4. Leonardo da Vinci was the proud owner of several cats which he liked to sketch. For homework, assign students the task of making a number of sketches of a pet or other animal. Share the sketches in class the next day. (A good resource for this activity is *Draw 50 Cats* by Lee J. Ames, Doubleday, 1986.)

5. See page 69 of Teacher Created Materials #288, *Explorers,* for additional projects that focus on Leonardo da Vinci.

Recommended Reading _____

The Annotated Mona Lisa by Carol Strickland, Ph.D., and John Boswell (Andrews and McMeel, 1992)

Leonardo da Vinci by Richard McLanathan (Harry N. Abrams, Inc., 1989)

Leonardo da Vinci by Ernest Raboff (Harper & Row, 1987)

The Life and Times of Leonardo da Vinci by Liana Bortolon (The Curtis Publishing Company, 1967)

Renaissance Painters Coloring Book by Andy Nelson (Culpepper Press, 1991)

Albrecht Dürer

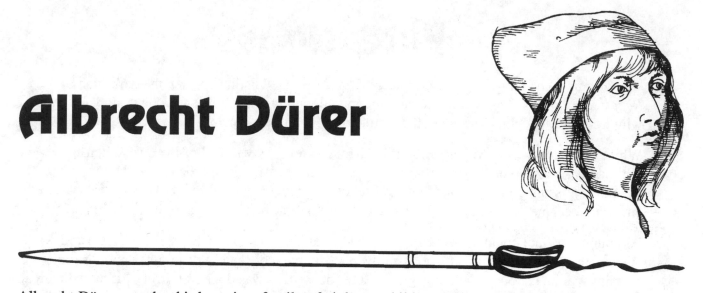

Albrecht Dürer was the third son in a family of eighteen children. His father was a goldsmith and his mother was the daughter of a goldsmith. It is fitting, then, that he spent his childhood working in his father's goldsmithing shop in Nuremberg, Germany. There he learned to make jewelry, statues, and pictures engraved in metal. When he was older, he traveled throughout Europe where he met other artists and studied great paintings. During his travels, Dürer kept drawing and watercolor sketch books of all that he saw. Albrecht was one of the first artists to meticulously record his travels.

Upon his return to Nuremberg, Dürer set up his own studio. Because of his interest in knowledge and his belief that art should be based on scientific observations, his pictures reflect details that most artists of the day failed to note. For example, his flowers accurately depict the difference between male and female plants. Portraits of people display the clothing and hair styles popular at that time. Animals are lifelike with every feature in place. Dürer respected and admired all forms of life and relied on direct observation rather than his memory to create his art works.

Artists before Albrecht Dürer were able to mass produce art works through wood cuts, a technique for making prints. The process follows these steps: First, a picture or design is drawn on a smooth block of wood. All but the outlines of the design are cut away leaving what is known as the relief. These relief lines are inked and pressed against paper. Numerous copies of an art work are thus possible. Dürer, however, took this technique to another level when he began to make engravings. Here, grooves were cut into a metal plate. Then ink was rubbed into the grooves and the plate's surface wiped clean. A press transferred the design to paper. One of Dürer's engravings, *Saint Jerome,* is especially lifelike. Lines are so delicately formed that it is difficult to believe it is a print and not a painting.

Albrecht also painted portraits. His first was of his father and was entitled *Dürer's Father;* this oil painting was more than 48" x 36" (122 cm x 90 cm) in size. Other portraits include a series of self-portraits beginning with the one he made when he was just thirteen years old.

A lifelong dedication to learning directly from nature led to his premature death in 1528. While walking through a swamp to view a whale, he contracted a fever which took his life. Dürer is still remembered for his lifelike drawings of animals and his attention to accurate detail.

Saint Jerome

Focus: Art should be based on scientific observation.

Activity: Creating a sandpaper print

Vocabulary: silverpoint; graphic art; wood cut; engraving

Art Lesson

Materials

✦ colored crayons
✦ fine grade sandpaper
✦ white construction paper
✦ electric iron
✦ towel

Directions

1. Review the steps in the engraving process. As a class, observe Dürer's engraving, *Saint Jerome.* Discuss with students the time involved in making such an intricate, detailed print. Establish that they are going to make prints but in a much simpler way.

2. Cut the sandpaper to half the size of the construction paper.

3. Direct students to use the crayons to draw an intricate design on the sandpaper.

4. Fold the paper in half and sandwich the sandpaper design between the halves.

5. Heat the iron to the cotton setting.

6. Place the towel over the construction paper sandwich and press firmly for 30 seconds.

7. Wait about five minutes before removing the sandpaper from the construction paper. Observe both prints. Display them together.

Extensions

1. Albrecht Dürer drew a number of self-portraits beginning with his first one at age 13. Compare the self-portrait he made of himself at this age with his *Self-Portrait* at age 29. (Both can be seen in Ernest Raboff's *Albrecht Dürer,* Harper & Row, 1988.) Discuss the techniques employed in each painting; note the attention to detail.

2. Students may enjoy making potato prints. Each student will need a potato half and a nail file or knife. In addition, you should have on hand liquid tempera paints in a variety of colors and white drawing paper.

    ✦ Cut each potato in half as shown to expose the most flesh.

    ✦ With the nail file or knife carve a design in the potato being careful to dig out potato around the shape desired.

    ✦ When the design is completed, dip the potato into a tempera color and immediately press onto paper.

    ✦ Repeat this last step as many times as desired. Be sure to wipe off the surface of the potato before changing tempera colors.

    For more printing activities see *The Print Book* by Diane James (Simon & Schuster, 1989).

3. Observe Dürer's drawing, *Hands of an Apostle.* Note the attention to detail and how lifelike they appear despite the absence of a body. Have students practice drawing hands.

    ✦ Direct students to place their non-writing hand on a sheet of white paper.

    ✦ With a pencil draw the outline of the hand.

    ✦ Fill in the hand with details to make it appear lifelike.

4. Leonardo da Vinci was one of Albrecht Dürer's contemporaries. Instruct students to compare the two artists by constructing a Venn diagram of their likenesses and differences.

Recommended Reading _____

Albrecht Dürer by Ernest Raboff (Harper & Row, 1988)

Famous Artists of the Past by Alice Elizabeth Chase (Platt & Munk, 1965)

Great Painters by Piero Ventura (G.P. Putnam's Sons, 1984)

Thomas Gainsborough

Thomas Gainsborough, born in 1727, became the ninth sibling in the Gainsborough household. His father, John, was a manufacturer of woolen cloth, hats, and clothes. He would have liked Thomas to learn the business but Thomas showed little interest in anything except drawing. Even in school, he would make drawings of flowers and leaves on the pages of his textbooks. Thomas' mother, Mary, understood her child's love of art as she, too, enjoyed painting flowers in her spare time.

Thomas would often take a holiday from school so he could go outdoors to draw; his father always gave his permission for these missed schooldays. One time, Thomas decided to write his own permission note. The writing looked exactly like his parent's. It probably would have gone unnoticed if the headmaster had not paid a surprise visit to the Gainsborough home after school. Thomas was ashamed of his actions and promised not to forge his father's handwriting again.

When Thomas was eleven years old, he was given some paints and brushes as a gift from his family. By the time he was twelve, he was ready to quit school to study painting. That chance did not come until he was fourteen when he was apprenticed to a London silversmith. There Thomas was introduced to a French engraver, Hubert Gravelot, who taught him the art of engraving. This helped him improve the lines in his drawings. Thomas also learned how to draw portraits using dolls as models.

At age nineteen, Gainsborough married Margaret Burr, a young woman he had met while on holiday to visit his family. After marrying, the couple moved to London and raised two daughters, Mary and Margaret. Thomas taught his girls to paint, but when they lost interest he gave lessons to his nephew, Gainsborough Dupont. The nephew went on to make his living as an artist but never achieved the fame of his uncle.

As the years progressed, Thomas Gainsborough grew tired and bored with painting portraits. His favorite subjects were landscapes which he painted in oils, or watercolors, or even crayons covered with heavy clear varnish. Nevertheless, he created some classic portraits, including those of all the members of King George III's family and that of the *Blue Boy*.

On August 2, 1788, Gainsborough succumbed to cancer. His had been a happy, fulfilling life for he had his wife and two daughters and a brilliant career as a portrait and landscape artist. In addition, he was a talented, self-taught musician who could play the violin, flute, bass violin, and harpsichord.

Blue Boy

Focus: It is not always necessary to paint according to the rules to create a beautiful painting.

Activity: Painting a portrait using one predominant color

Vocabulary: landscape; seascape; portrait

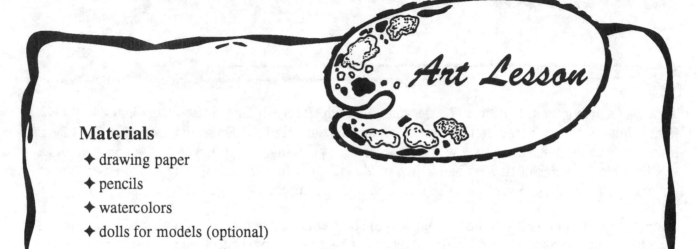

Materials

✦ drawing paper

✦ pencils

✦ watercolors

✦ dolls for models (optional)

Directions

1. Ask students to examine closely the picture of *Blue Boy.* Ask students to explain the appropriateness of the picture's title. Have them describe the texture of the boy's clothing. Discuss the effect of the dark background as contrasted with the blue foreground.

2. Set up the dolls as models or have students choose a picture from a magazine or a family photo to copy.

3. In pencil, have students sketch the outlines of the subject.

4. With the watercolors, ask students to paint the subject in shades of the same color.

5. Allow students to make up titles for the finished paintings.

Extensions

1. On numerous occasions, Thomas Gainsborough met Joshua Reynolds, another famous portrait artist of the era. Find some samples of Joshua Reynolds' work and compare them to those of Gainsborough. How are they similar? How are they different?

2. A rich ironmonger asked Gainsborough to paint a full-length portrait of his son, Jonathan Buttall. Usually Gainsborough did not allow his subjects to wear fancy clothes; he preferred that they wear their normal attire. Ask students to speculate why Gainsborough had Jonathan wear the shiny satin suit for the portrait. Discuss why they think *Blue Boy* is such a popular painting.

3. Thomas Gainsborough taught his two daughters to paint landscapes by building models in his study. He would use coal for rocks, sand, dried grass, pebbles, a mirror for a lake, and broccoli for the trees. Group the students and direct each group to create a landscape employing the same materials that Gainsborough did. After they have completed the landscape, tell them to draw a paper-and-pencil sketch of the scene. Display the sketches with the proper 3-D models.

4. Thomas and Mary Gainsborough adored their two daughters Mary and Margaret. The sisters were the subject of some of Thomas' paintings including *The Painter's Daughters Chasing a Butterfly*. To better understand this piece read about it in the book *The Story in a Picture: Children in Art* by Robin Richmond (Ideals Children's Books, 1992).

5. Gainsborough had an odd habit of inviting people home with him so he could paint their portraits. One time, he was approached by a beggar woman and her small son. Gainsborough gave her a few coins and then told the woman he wanted to take the boy home with him so he could paint his portrait. The woman agreed and the boy was taken to the Gainsborough household. A few days later, he ran away to find his mother and Tom went out to find the lad. Once again, he brought the boy to his house and once again the boy ran away. After relaying this story to the students, have them write an original story about a person that Thomas Gainsborough invited to his home to sit for a portrait.

Recommended Reading _____

The Book of Art. Vol. 6. British and North American Art to 1900, ed. by Dr. Kenneth Garlick (Grolier Incorporated, 1965)

Great Lives edited by Simon Boughton (Grisewood & Dempsey, 1988)

A History of Art by Marshall B. Davidson (Random House, 1984)

17th and 18th Century Art adapted by Ariane Ruskin (McGraw-Hill, 1969)

Thomas Gainsborough: Artist of England by Sally Glendinning (Garrard Publishing Company, 1969)

Michelangelo

Michelangelo, whose full name was Michelangelo Buonarroti, was born on March 6, 1475. As an infant, Michelangelo was sent to live with a stonecutter and his wife. It was there that he probably learned to see the forms within stone in a way that no other person ever has.

Although Michelangelo began school at the age of seven, his mind and heart were focused on art. When he was 13, Michelangelo was finally allowed to join the painting workshop of the Ghirlandaio brothers. The young boy's talent soon became obvious to the brothers, and instead of charging him for lessons, they paid him for his work. After his three-year internship, Michelangelo went on to study sculpture at the garden of Lorenzo de' Medici, the actual ruler of Florence. In time, Lorenzo became Michelangelo's first patron. After Lorenzo's death in 1492, a grieving Michelangelo went to the monastery hospital of Santo Spirito in Florence to work with the dead. Like Leonardo da Vinci, Michelangelo wanted to learn about the human body's systems, organs, muscles, and skeleton. He would use this knowledge to create his many paintings and carved statues.

In 1497, Michelangelo was summoned to Rome. The Roman Catholic church was very wealthy and could provide him with money to continue his work. There he was commissioned to make a statue for the pope's church. The resulting *Pietà* (Italian for pity) depicts the dead Christ lying across his mother Mary's lap. It is carved from marble, yet its delicacy suggests it is done in cloth. This masterpiece is even more amazing when one realizes that Michelangelo was only 23 years old at the time, and he was given only one year to carve the figures.

When he returned to Florence, Michelangelo was commissioned to do the famous 14-foot (4 m) statue of the Biblical figure, David. In this statue, a young David is shown with a slingshot about to kill the giant Goliath. In 1500, Michelangelo was called back to Rome by Pope Julius who wanted statues sculpted for his tomb. Before they could be started, however, the pope changed priorities wanting the ceiling of the Sistine Chapel painted. Four years later this masterpiece with its 300 figures was finished. The work had been grueling and Michelangelo and Pope Julius had argued heavily over its completion. Working conditions had been dangerous and lonely. Today the Sistine Chapel ceiling is considered one of the wonders of the world.

During his remaining years, Michelangelo continued to sculpt, paint, design buildings and write poetry. He lived to a remarkable age of almost ninety and died February 18, 1564.

Pietà

Focus: Michelangelo could see figures in the stone before carving began.

Activity: Sculpting a figure

Vocabulary: Fresco; Carrara quarry; sculpture

Art Lesson

Materials

- ✦ small cooking pot
- ✦ wooden spoon
- ✦ hot plate or other heat source
- ✦ one cup (250 mL) of sand (available in art supply stores)
- ✦ one-half cup (125 mL) of cornstarch
- ✦ one teaspoon (5 mL) powdered alum
- ✦ three-fourths cup (180 mL) of hot water

Directions

1. As a class, observe the flowing movement of the cloth on Michelangelo's figures. Discuss the details of the carving that make it appear so lifelike.

2. Prepare the modeling dough using the directions below. This recipe yields approximately two cups (500 mL) of dough. Adjust the recipe to make enough for all the students.

   - ✦ Combine the four ingredients in the pot and mix well.
   - ✦ Stir constantly over medium heat until the mixture becomes thick in consistency; allow to cool thoroughly.
   - ✦ Mold the dough into lifelike figures.
   - ✦ Air dry the completed figures for 3 to 4 days.

3. Provide each student with enough modeling dough to create his or her own sculpture. Allow students to exhibit and explain their masterpieces.

Extensions

1. Introduce the study of Michelangelo by viewing the film, *The Agony and the Ecstasy,* or by reading aloud the book, *Michael the Angel* by Laura Fischetto (Doubleday, 1993).

2. The Sistine Chapel was painted using a *fresco technique* in which paint is applied directly to the walls or ceiling. Paints are made by grinding minerals found in the ground and mixing with distilled water. Then the paints are applied onto a wet plaster surface. These surfaces contain lime, which when mixed with paint causes a chemical reaction. The only way to remove the paint is with a hammer!

    Have students discuss the possible problems Michelangelo might have encountered while using this method. Record the responses on chart paper. Then have them research the actual problems. A good source for information on this topic is the book, *Introducing Michelangelo* by Robin Richmond (Little, Brown & Company, 1992).

3. Give students a choice between Michelangelo and Leonardo da Vinci as the greatest artist who ever lived. Direct them to write at least five different reasons for their choice. Share the writings in small groups.

4. To paint the ceiling of the Sistine Chapel, Michelangelo constructed a special stool which he could lean against and rest his head while he worked. Students can simulate this back-breaking experience with the following idea: Have each student tape a sheet of paper to the underside of the desk. Direct students to lie on the floor underneath their desks so they can reach up to paint a picture. Markers or crayons are recommended for this project.

5. The ceiling of the Sistine Chapel which Michelangelo painted was 132 feet (40 m) long by 46 feet (14 m) wide. To help students visualize the magnitude of this project, do the following. Using yarn or string have the students measure an outdoor area 132 feet by 46 feet (40 m x 14 m). When it is completed, tell the students to stand inside and move around in the space.

6. For more activities on Michelangelo, see page 69 of Teacher Created Materials #288, *Explorers*.

Recommended Reading _____

The Cambridge Introduction to Art: The Renaissance by Rosa Maria Letts, (Cambridge University Press, 1981)

Famous People by Kenneth and Valerie McLeish (Troll Associates, 1991)

I Carve Stone by Joan Fine (Thomas Y. Crowell, 1979)

Introducing Michelangelo by Robin Richmond (Little, Brown & Company, 1992)

The Life and Times of Michelangelo by Maria Luisa Rizzatti (The Curtis Publishing Company, 1967)

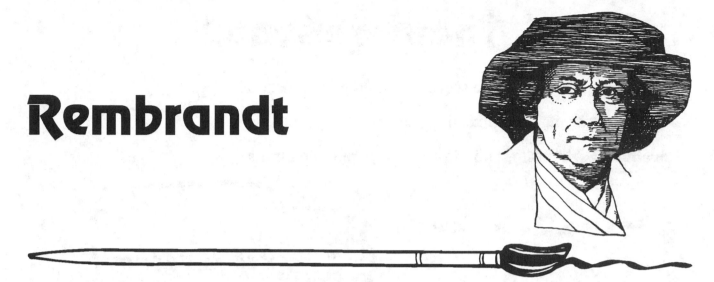

Rembrandt

One unique accomplishment sets Rembrandt apart from his contemporaries: He rendered nearly one hundred self-portraits over the course of forty years. Not until van Gogh did any other artist explore his own image with quite the same dedication.

Rembrandt Harmensz van Rijn was born on July 15, 1606; he was the eighth of nine children. His father, Harmen, was a miller whose work consisted of grinding wheat into fine flour for bread. Rembrandt's mother, Cornelia, was the daughter of a baker. When he was fifteen, Rembrandt began to study painting and by the age of twenty-three had reached the master painter level. At twenty-five, he was already established professionally in Amsterdam. For the first twenty years of his career, his portraits were the height of fashion; Rembrandt was deluged with requests for sittings. Sometimes he could be difficult to work with and did not like to be rushed. Many patrons resorted to bribery just so they might receive their portraits on time.

During this popular time of his life, Rembrandt married Saskin. She eventually bore him a son, Titus, who lived to adulthood; their other children had died earlier. Rembrandt's wealth enabled him to buy fine clothes and to fill his house with beautiful rare furnishings. He also began to purchase and collect the paintings of other well-known painters. The artist enjoyed his popularity until 1642, when his beloved wife died unexpectedly. It was during this time that Rembrandt's paintings took on a more somber tone and were dominated by reds and browns. In that same year, he lost public favor after painting *The Night Watch*. Several gentleman had paid the same amount to be portrayed in this scene, yet Rembrandt chose to highlight only some of the members. Rembrandt's public turned against him.

The remaining years of his life were spent struggling against poverty. By 1656, he was forced to declare bankruptcy. He sold his house, his art collection, and his sumptuous furnishings and moved to the poor Jewish area of Amsterdam. Rembrandt continued to receive some commissions until 1667; he died in October of 1669 at the age of 63.

Today Rembrandt is remembered for many accomplishments. He used Impressionism years before Monet and Renoir would explore the same style. His portraits revealed two sides of the sitter's personalities — one side was bathed in light while the other side's features were hidden in the shadows. Rembrandt was regarded as a very accomplished etcher. Perhaps Rembrandt is best known for his prolific collection of over four hundred paintings.

The Nightwatch

Focus: Rembrandt's group scenes featured physical action.

Activity: Drawing a group action scene

Vocabulary: Impasto; Old Master; "corporation portraits"

Art Lesson

Materials

✦ drawing paper
✦ pencils

Directions

1. Have students examine *The Nightwatch* and observe the feeling of movement evoked in the picture. Ask students to describe the action. Encourage them to explain how Rembrandt achieves this feeling.

2. Watch a group action event on the playground — a ball game, a race, etc. If necessary, have groups of students in the class stage an action event. Rotate the groups so that every child has a chance to participate in and observe action.

3. Direct the students to draw a picture of what they have observed. Encourage students to use shading to convey a feeling of movement. (For more information about shading see *I Draw. I Paint. Colored Pencils* by Isidro Sanchez, Barron's Educational Series, Inc., 1991.)

28

Extensions

1. Rembrandt is regarded as an elite member of a group of artists known as the "Old Masters." Have students research and learn about some of the other artists in that group. (For a partial listing of "Old Masters" see page 32.)

2. Over a forty-year period, Rembrandt produced nearly one hundred self-portraits. Students can create their own portfolio collection with this assignment.

    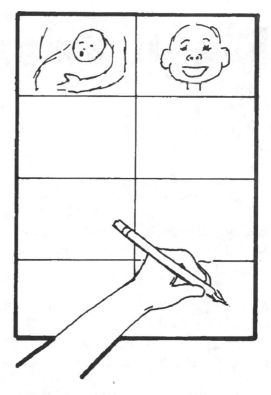

    ✦ Give each student a sheet of drawing paper or copy paper.

    ✦ Tell students to fold the papers in half, and then in half again, to make eight equal sections when unfolded.

    ✦ In each square, the students are to draw a portrait of themselves at a different age. (They may want to bring in some photographs of themselves at various ages.) The first square should reflect infancy, and the last square should be a present-day picture.

3. Examine some of Rembrandt's portraits to see how he revealed the two sides of a subject's personality. For example, have the students look at Rembrandt's self-portrait done around the year 1629. Cover one side of the face and have students describe what they see. Now cover the other side of the face; what do the students observe? Group the students and have them try this method with some of Rembrandt's other portraits. Tell them to explain what they think the artist is really saying about himself.

4. After Rembrandt's wife, Saskin, died in 1642, his style evolved and changed to what is known as his late style. Assign a group of students to compare the artist's early style with his late style. One fine resource for this activity is *The Annotated Mona Lisa* by Carol Strickland, Ph.D., and John Boswell (Andrews and McMeel, 1992). Have this group of students create a chart and present their findings to the whole class.

5. Introduce Rembrandt by reading aloud the intriguing story, *Rembrandt's Beret* by Johnny Alcorn (Tambourine Books, 1991). Assign students to write their own Rembrandt adventure after researching more about him.

Recommended Reading _____

Lives of the Artists by M.B. Goffstein (Farrar, Straus, Giroux, 1981)

Rembrandt by Ernest Raboff (Harper & Row, 1987)

Rembrandt by Mike Venezia (Children's Press, 1988)

17th and 18th Century Art by Ariane Ruskin (McGraw-Hill, 1969)

A Weekend with Rembrandt by Pascal Bonafoux (Rizzoli International Publications, 1991)

Diego Velázquez

His full name is Diego Rodriguez de Silva y Velázquez, but he is more commonly known as Diego Velázquez. Born in Seville, Spain, on June 6, 1599, Diego was destined to become Spain's most outstanding artist.

As a child, Velázquez showed great artistic ability and his parents wanted him to study with master painter Francisco Herrera. Instead, Diego chose to join the studio of Francesco Pacheco where he would be allowed more artistic freedom. In addition, Diego studied literature and philosophy. When Diego was twenty years old, he married Herrera's daughter, Juana. Together they had two daughters.

Velázquez' first three portraits of King Philip IV were so successful that at age twenty-five, he was appointed to be the Royal Painter. Life at court was a privileged time for Diego and his family. During his lifetime stay there, Diego became a friend as well as an advisor to the king.

King Philip IV first ascended to the throne when he was only sixteen years old and for the next 20 years he was dominated by his chamberlain, Duke Olivares. Olivares had a grim temperament. He was said to have laughed only three times in his life. The Duke's personal life was beset with tragedies. His first wife and most of his children died. The one surviving heir was both physically and mentally impaired. To offset the melancholy tone of the court, jesters and dwarfs lived on the premises to provide a diversion. Dwarfs can be seen in some of Velázquez' paintings such as _Maids of Honor_ and _Don Antonio El Ingles_. In all cases, Diego portrayed his subjects with equal dignity and respect.

Today, Diego Velázquez is regarded as an outstanding Spanish artist and a great innovator. He demonstrated his talents when he brought natural composition to his paintings and set his models in more natural poses. He also created forms through the use of color and light rather than lines. In addition, Velázquez used loose brush strokes which when viewed up close tended to melt into dabs of color. From afar the result was a definite figure. The result of these techniques was a startlingly real image of the human figure. Diego Velázquez died in 1660 at the age of 61.

Prince Philip Prosper

Focus: Velázquez preferred to use color and light rather than lines to create forms.

Activity: Using dabs of color to paint a typical child

Vocabulary: Baroque; composition; loose brush strokes

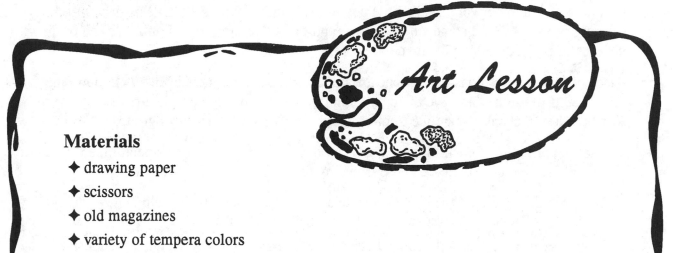

Materials

✦ drawing paper

✦ scissors

✦ old magazines

✦ variety of tempera colors

✦ paint brushes

Directions

1. Ask students to closely examine the painting, *Prince Philip Prosper.* See if students can discern any lines in the picture or if they can see how the light and dark colors are used to create forms.

2. Let students look through magazines to find an appropriate child as a model for their painting. Have them cut out the picture.

3. Place the picture conspicuously so that it can be referred to during the painting process.

4. Remind students that Velázquez did not use lines to create his forms.

5. Direct the students to use short brush strokes with the tempera paints to make a picture of the child.

Extensions

1. Juan de Pareja was a servant and pupil of Diego. Juan ground paints, cleaned brushes, and on occasion acted as a traveling companion. When Juan was forty-five, he surprised Diego with a series of fine paintings he had created himself. To learn more about his association with one of Spain's most famous artists, assign the students to read the Newbery winning book *I, Juan de Pareja* by Elizabeth Barton de Trevino (listed in the Recommended Reading below).

2. Compare the clothing worn by the little boy in the painting *Prince Philip Prosper*, with the typical clothing of today. Have some students do a report on other dress styles of the period or draw pictures of typical clothing for that era.

3. Diego Velázquez was considered to be a Baroque artist. Direct the students to find out the definition of Baroque and have them research the life of another Baroque artist such as Rembrandt or Rubens. Share the findings in whole class or within small groups.

4. If possible, bring in a Dutch Masters cigar box to class and have students determine the identity of the painters pictured there. Choose from any of the following assignments.

    ✦ Have a group of student volunteers create costumes and pose as the "old Dutch masters." Or, create a modern version and pose as the "new Dutch masters."

    ✦ Write any or all of the following names on the chalkboard. Let the students choose a name from this list. Direct them to find out five facts about their chosen person. Compile the lists into a class book; display for all to read.

Botticelli	Dürer	Michelangelo	Titian
Bruegel	El Greco	Raphael	Van Dyck
Caravaggio	Hals	Rembrandt	Van Eyck
da Vinci	La Tour	Rubens	Velázquez

    ✦ Have students write a story about any two of the above listed painters. It could be a tale about the day they met, or the words they exchanged about one another's painting, or a comparison of their lives and work.

Recommended Reading _____

Diego Rodriguez de Silva y Velázquez by Ernest Raboff (J.B. Lippincott, 1988)

Great Painters by Piero Ventura (G.P. Putnam's Sons, 1984)

I, Juan de Pareja by Elizabeth Barton de Trevino (Farrar, Straus and Giroux, 1965)

17th and 18th Century Art by Ariane Ruskin (McGraw-Hill, 1969)

Elisabeth Vigee-Lebrun

Her full name was Marie Louise Elisabeth Vigee-Lebrun, but she is more commonly known as Elisabeth Vigee-Lebrun. By the time Elisabeth was fifteen years old, she had already developed a skillful technique and had achieved some notoriety. It was her father, a portrait artist, who inspired her to become a painter.

Elisabeth became famous when she began to paint a series of portraits of Marie Antoinette, the Queen of France. During this time, the two became friends; they even sang duets together. Elisabeth's paintings were done from a woman's perspective. She always made sure to picture her subjects at their fashionable best. It soon became popular among the French nobility to have a portrait painted by this beautiful young woman. Because of her fame she was invited into the French Royal Academy of Painting, one of only three women inducted into this prestigious society at this time. There she could study art and also have her work shown.

When the French Revolution began in 1789, Paris was no longer safe for anyone who had close ties to the royal family. Marie Antoinette was arrested and Elisabeth feared for her own and her daughter's lives. The two disguised themselves as workers and fled to Italy. Elisabeth was forced to leave unfinished paintings behind.

In Italy, Vigee-Lebrun was welcomed by the people who knew of her reputation. Many of them commissioned her to paint their portraits. For many years, she traveled throughout Europe painting royal portraits in each city she visited. During her lifetime, she painted an amazing 900 portraits. Unfortunately, she did not become wealthy from her work because her husband, art dealer Jean-Baptiste Lebrun, gambled and lost much of her hard-earned money. Eventually the two separated.

Before Elisabeth left Italy she was asked by the Uffizi Gallery to paint a self-portrait. The resulting picture shows a beautiful woman of thirty-five. Today it is part of that gallery's unique collection of portraits. When she finally grew tired of wandering, Elisabeth was able to return home to France, which by then was ruled by Napoleon. It was there that she died in 1842. Elisabeth Vigee-Lebrun had devoted her life to art and is considered to be one of the best portrait painters of the late 18th century to early 19th century.

Self-Portrait

Focus: Portray subjects at their best.

Activity: Drawing a portrait

Vocabulary: portrait; commissioned

Art Lesson

Materials

- ✦ pencils
- ✦ drawing paper or typing paper
- ✦ costumes or old dress-up clothes

Directions

1. Encourage students to observe the detail in Elisabeth Vigee-Lebrun's portrait (the delicate texture of the lace, the sheen of the satin, etc.). Ask the students to describe the artist based on her picture. (e.g., Do they think she is kind, old, happy, etc?)

2. Pair the students. Have one partner dress up and become the subject while the other partner is the artist.

3. The artist may choose the costume or clothes for his subject and then may pose him.

4. Using pencil, have students sketch a portrait of the subject.

5. When the portrait is complete the two partners switch roles.

Extensions

1. While Elisabeth Vigee-Lebrun managed to escape the French Revolution unharmed, the members of the royal family were not so lucky. Group students and let them choose from among the following topics.

    ✦ Research the French Revolution and its causes. Include in their report a definition of the terms *States-General* and *Third Estate.*

    ✦ Find out why Marie Antoinette was so unpopular. What was she referring to when she said to let the people eat cake? What happened to Marie Antoinette?

    ✦ Describe the philosophy of the Enlightenment. What was its role in the French Revolution?

    ✦ Who was Napoleon? What was the Napoleonic Empire?

2. Have students find pictures of Marie Antoinette and other key figures of the French Revolution. Observe their clothing. If possible, find a book that shows clothing of all the classes. Compare the workers' clothes to those of the royal family. Direct the students to draw a picture of a typical working-class wardrobe.

3. Elisabeth Vigee-Lebrun wrote memoirs of her life. These notes give us an insight into life in Europe at that time in history, plus they provide evidence of Elisabeth's personality. In one account, for example, she told about the day her daughter was born. She explained that she stayed in her studio and continued to work between labor pains.

    ✦ Memoirs are an important part of history because they provide valuable glimpses into everyday life. They provide glimpses that history books often leave out. Direct students to write memoirs of their typical days starting from the time they get up in the morning until they go to school and arrive home again. Save the writings in a class book. Bury them in a time capsule for future classes to dig up.

4. Elisabeth worked with crude brushes that were fashioned of tufts of fur or hair attached to a stick. Challenge students to create their own paintbrushes using craft sticks, feathers, fabric scraps, or other available material. Have them paint a few strokes with each brush and compare the designs they make.

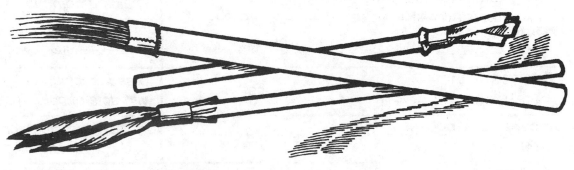

Recommended Reading _____

Academic American Encyclopedia, Vol. 19 (Grolier Incorporated, 1990)

History of Women Artists for Children by Vivian Sheldon Epstein (VSE Publisher, 1987)

The Self-Portrait in Art by Sharon Lerner (Lerner Publications, 1965)

Nineteenth Century Artists

The nineteenth century saw a dramatic change in civilization as the church lost its control and monarchies were toppled. New forces such as industrialization and urbanization brought about cities filled with dissatisfied poor. Science knowledge progressed at an amazing rate and brought numerous changes with it. In the meantime, the art world was experiencing some radical changes, too. While formerly one style of painting would dominate the scene for centuries, now smaller, short-term trends began to emerge.

At the beginning of the century, there were three major trends which competed with one another — Neoclassicism, Romanticism, and Realism. Later in the century, these were replaced with Impressionism, Post-Impressionism, and Symbolism. It is not surprising that this time period is known as the birth of the "isms"!

Below is a listing of the artists represented in this section. Following each name and country of origin is a brief statement indicating particularly noteworthy achievements.

Artist	Country of Origin	Achievements
Rosa Bonheur (1822-1899)	France	*one of the leading painters of animals of her time*
Mary Cassatt (1844-1926)	U.S.A./France	*known for her paintings of mothers and children*
George Catlin (1796-1872)	U.S.A.	*painter who documented the Native American*
Edgar Degas (1834-1917)	France	*specialized in capturing movement in a figure*
Claude Monet (1840-1926)	France	*developed the technique of using short dabs of paint*
Edvard Munch (1863-1944)	Norway	*forerunner of Expressionism; painted from his emotions*
Henri Rousseau (1844-1910)	Norway	*first and greatest of the primitive painters*
Georges Seurat (1859-1891)	France	*used technique of painting with dots of color (pointillism)*
Vincent van Gogh (1853-1890)	Holland	*probably the most reproduced painter in history*

Rosa Bonheur

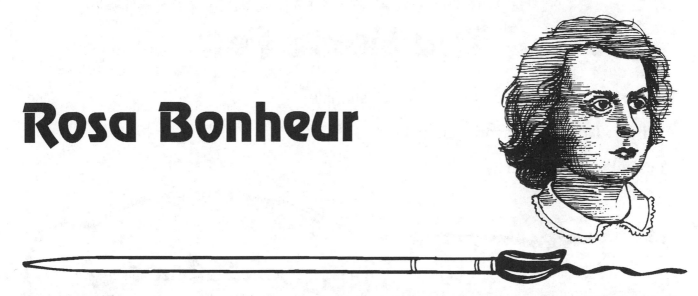

From the time she was a child, Marie Rosalie Bonheur led an independent and unusual lifestyle. Rosa, as she was more commonly known, was born in 1822 in Bordeaux, France. Her father, Raymond, was an artist himself, and he taught art to Rosa and her three other siblings. Mr. Bonheur instilled in Rosa the belief that women could do and be anything they chose for themselves.

As a child, Rosa kept a pet sheep on the balcony of the family's sixth-floor apartment. The sheep had to be carried downstairs by her brothers every day so that it could get some exercise. Rosa grew up to sketch sheep and other animals which she loved so passionately. She observed animals everywhere — the fair, the countryside, and even at horse auctions. Her keen observations are reflected in her paintings.

In 1889, Buffalo Bill's Wild West Show camped outside of Paris for seven months during part of its European tour. The entourage was comprised of 115 Native Americans, 48 cowboys, 6 cowgirls, 6 vaqueros (Mexican cowboys), 20 buffalo, 25 mustangs, 8 dogs, and 186 horses. Rosa visited the camp and produced a number of interesting scenes of William F. Cody and his group.

Rosa was to become one of the nineteenth century's leading painters of animals. With the money she earned from her work, she was able to purchase a large home complete with a studio. The property even contained a farm for her many animals which included goats, chickens, peacocks, and dogs. When she wanted to learn more about animal anatomy, she took a job at a slaughterhouse. This knowledge gave her animal pictures an added accuracy. To observe horses without drawing any attention to herself, Rosa dressed in men's clothing and attended the Paris horse market.
Soon her animal paintings had made her so popular that a "Rosa Bonheur" doll was created for young girls. Rosa became one of the most popular female artists of the nineteenth century and was awarded numerous medals from kings and queens in European countries to reward her for her realistic renditions of animals. In 1865, she became the first woman to be awarded the Grand Cross of the Legion of Honour (a French award).

Rosa's personal life continued to be unconventional. She rejected the idea of marriage to a man and lived with her friend Nathalie Micas for forty years. Her hair was cut short like a man's, and she obtained a police permit to allow her to wear trousers. Rosa also smoked cigarettes and was an outspoken feminist. This colorful character maintained her place as one of the most successful female painters of the 1800s, and she no doubt inspired many other women to pursue an art career.

The Horse Fair

Focus: Rosa Bonheur had a passion for animals.

Activity: Drawing a favorite animal

Vocabulary: Realism

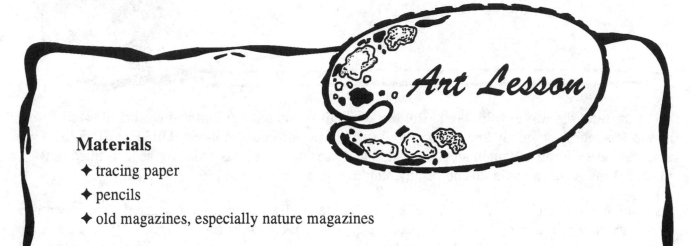

Materials
- ✦ tracing paper
- ✦ pencils
- ✦ old magazines, especially nature magazines

Directions

1. Locate pictures of animals in old magazines. Note whether the pictures depict the realism of the animals. Ask students to tell what Rosa did to bring such realism to the painting. Discuss the features which give the animals this "alive" look.

2. Let the students choose a favorite animal picture from one of the magazines.

3. Direct students to use a pencil to trace the outline of the animal.

4. Encourage students to add shadows, shading, and other details to give the picture realism. For more information about shading, see the book *Draw!* by Kim Solga (F&W Publications, Inc., 1991) or the November/December issue of *Learning 88 Magazine* which contains a pull-out poster.

Extensions

1. Follow up the art lesson on page 38 with a lesson on drawing horses. For additional information about this topic, see *I Can Draw Horses* by Gill Spiers (Simon & Schuster, 1983).

2. Assign students to find out what is inside their favorite animals. Tell them to choose an animal, research it, and draw a picture of its skeleton. Or, draw the internal organs and label them. An excellent resource for this activity is *What's Inside? Small Animals* by Angela Royston (Dorling Kindersley, 1991). Other titles in this series include *Insects* and *Animal Homes*.

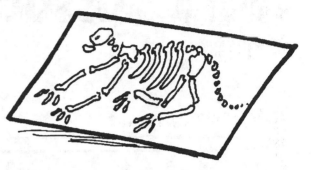

3. Because Bonheur's work was so popular a "Rosa Bonheur" doll was marketed for little girls. Have students draw a picture of the doll based on the descriptions they have read about Rosa's hairstyle and clothing.

4. Read about the life and times of Rosa Bonheur in the books *Rosa Bonheur* by Robyn Turner (Little, Brown & Company, 1991) or *History of Women Artists for Children* by Vivian Sheldon Epstein (VSE Publishers, 1987).

5. Some of Rosa Bonheur's actions were unusual and shocking for the times. Her hair was cut short like a man's and she wore trousers. Women of those days wore long hair and long skirts. Have students choose from either of the two writing assignments below.

   ✦ You are a newspaper reporter and you have been assigned to ask Rosa about her unusual behaviors. Write an interview including the questions you might have for her and the answers as you think she may have answered them.

   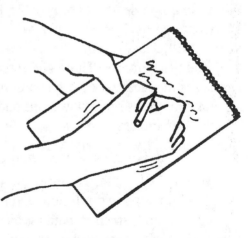

   ✦ Rosa Bonheur was an outspoken advocate of women's rights. Find out what rights women had in the 19th century; make a list of them. Make another list of rights that women have today. Compare the two lists. In which century would the students prefer to have lived? Explain.

Recommended Reading _____

History of Women Artists for Children by Vivian Sheldon Epstein (VSE Publishers, 1987)

Rosa Bonheur by Robyn Turner (Little, Brown & Company, 1991)

Mary Cassatt

Mary Cassatt was able to achieve in her lifetime something that many artists never experience — recognition as a great artist. It was a well-deserved honor, one that did not come easily for Mary. Women in the nineteenth century were discouraged from pursuing a career in art. They were not allowed to look at or use nude models to help them learn basic drawing techniques. Instead, some life-drawing classes for women in 1859 substituted live cows for human models. During the same time period women artists were made unwelcome at social gatherings where male artists were free to discuss new and innovative ideas. Despite these obstacles, Mary determined that art was to be her life.

The beginnings of her passion were probably in Paris when her family moved to improve their status. Exposure to the Louvre and other large art museums opened her eyes to a new and beautiful world. After the tragic death of her brother, Robbie, the family returned home to America. At the age of 16, Mary entered the Pennsylvania Academy of the Fine Arts in Philadelphia where she studied for four years. Still, Mary felt that her education was lacking and that she needed to study in Paris; in 1866, she sailed for France. There she discovered even more restrictions were put on women than at the Pennsylvania Academy. A resourceful Mary soon learned how to bypass these rules, and she began copying paintings on her own. In addition, she took private art lessons and attended informal schools which offered classes for women only. Two years later, when war with Prussia broke out with France, Mary reluctantly returned to live with her family in Pennsylvania.

The year 1871 brought some fortuitous changes to Mary's life. She was commissioned by a bishop in Pittsburgh to copy two religious paintings in Parma, Italy. While there, she studied the artist, Correggio, and learned to paint subjects from many points of view. From Italy, Mary went to Spain and while studying everyday Spanish life, she also learned to make her subjects appear almost real through the use of contrast. Sometime in April of 1873, Mary returned to Paris where she befriended Edgar Degas. At his invitation, she exhibited her work with a group called the Independents, an art group who rejected conventional art in favor of capturing their immediate impressions of what they saw. Because of this method of painting what they saw and felt, artists like Cassatt and Degas became known as Impressionists.

Mary Cassatt's career ended with her death in 1926 at age 82. During her lifetime, she received many honors, including the distinguished Medal of Honor from the French government and two U.S. postage stamps — one a portrait of Mary and the other a reproduction of her painting, *The Boating Party*.

Little Girl in a Blue Armchair

Focus: In her paintings, Mary Cassatt tried to capture the changes in light on her subjects.

Activity: Creating an Impressionist painting

Vocabulary: Impressionist; genre; oils; pastels

Art Lesson

Materials
+ newspapers
+ white construction paper
+ old toothbrushes
+ tempera or poster paints
+ pieces of screen

Directions

1. Discuss with the students Mary Cassatt's style of painting, particularly that shown in *Little Girl in a Blue Armchair*. Point out the relaxed pose and the way light is reflected in different portions of the painting.

2. Tell the students to spread newspaper over their working surface.

3. Place the construction paper in the middle of the newspaper.

4. Have students dip the toothbrushes into the paint with one hand and hold the screen above the surface of the construction paper with the other.

5. Brush the surface of the screen with the toothbrush to spatter paint onto the paper's surface.

6. Repeat the process using a number of colors. Draw designs onto the background when dry (optional).

Extensions

1. Read *Mary Cassatt* by Robyn Montana Turner (Little, Brown & Company, 1992). This first-rate biography tells the fascinating story of Mary and her family and her passion for art. Readers are treated to a visual feast of some of Cassatt's most famous paintings. Artistic terms are described in an understanding manner and the various phases of Mary's paintings are gracefully unfolded within the story line.

2. Study photographs of mothers and their children. Try to read the feelings and emotions expressed by parent and child. Practice reading pictures found in magazines before looking at personal photos.

   ◆ Compare and contrast two or more photos; how are they alike? different?

   ◆ Brainstorm a list of adjectives that describe the emotions conveyed in a particular photo.

   ◆ Cut out pictures of mothers and their children from magazines. Give each student, or student pair, a picture. Tell them to write a story describing what is happening in the picture or have them tell what they think the mother and child are feeling at that moment.

3. Edgar Degas was one of Mary Cassatt's contemporaries and most staunch supporter. Find out more about this artist and his style of painting.

4. Mary Cassatt belonged to a group of artists known as the Impressionists. Ask students what is meant by that term; have them research the word if they do not know its meaning. Tell them to make a list of other Impressionists of that time period.

5. Describe how attitudes towards women have changed since Mary Cassatt was first determined to become an artist.

   ◆ Ask students to describe what their fathers might say to them if they announced they would like to pursue an art career.

   ◆ Have the students write a conversation they might have with a parent who objected to their desire to become an artist. How would they convince someone that they really want to become an artist?

Recommended Reading _____

"Mary's Impressions," *Highlights for Children,* April 1993 issue, pages 16-17

Mary Cassatt by Michael Cain (Chelsea House, 1989)

Mary Cassatt by Robyn Montana Turner (Little, Brown & Company, 1992)

Masterpieces of American Art: A Fact-Filled Coloring Book by Alan Gartenhaus (Running Press, 1992)

George Catlin

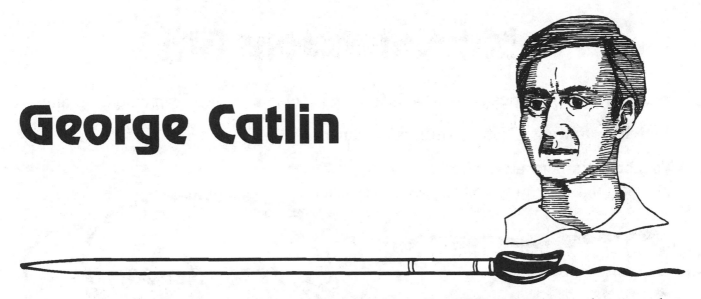

Certainly there were other talented painters of the Native American West in the nineteenth century, but none portrayed the Native Americans with more respect and dignity than that shown by artist George Catlin. For years he traveled along the Missouri and Mississippi Rivers and in present-day Oklahoma to observe and study almost fifty different tribes. By 1837, he had gathered information and artifacts about theses cultures and had completed 500 portraits and sketches which he compiled into an exhibition called "Catlin's Indian Gallery." Concerned that the Native American way of life was endangered, he was determined to preserve their customs by providing a permanent record of them.

George Catlin was born into a prosperous family in Wilkes-Barre, Pennsylvania, on July 26, 1796, the fifth of fourteen children. Poor health forced Mr. Catlin to abandon his legal practice in Connecticut and move the family to the wilderness in Broome County in New York State. It was in this setting that a ten-year-old George first saw and befriended a Native American named Oneida. When Oneida was found dead some days later, it was a memory that was to stay with George forever.

Despite his father's parent's protests, George attended law school. It was here that he read about the Native Americans, studied science, and completed his first small portraits. For a few years he actually practiced law, but then one day he gave it up to pursue his art career. He had no formal training and was completely self-taught, but that did not stop him from exhibiting and becoming a popular artist.

In 1828, Catlin met and married Clara Gregory, the daughter of a wealthy Albany family. He soon left her with her family while he began his odyssey to record Native American customs and culture. They would get together between his travels and even managed to have a family of three daughters and one son. Through it all, Clara was the one who encouraged and supported her husband faithfully.

After he had produced this magnificent collection of Native American portraits and artifacts, Catlin tried to sell his Indian Gallery to the United States Senate. When they turned him down, he packed up his exhibit and headed for London. There he met with some early success, but expenses were high and he lived beyond his means. His wife and family joined him, but before they could return to America Clara died of pneumonia; later that year, his beloved son, George, died of typhoid.

For fifteen more years, Catlin remained in Europe. His daughters had long been returned to America by concerned relatives. Failing health finally forced him to return to New York where his daughters took care of him until he died on December 23, 1872.

Mint, a Pretty Girl

Focus: Native Americans are proud, dignified people with their own unique culture.

Activity: Drawing a Native American costume

Vocabulary: portrait; artifact

Art Lesson

Materials

- ✦ brown paper bags
- ✦ scissors
- ✦ pencils
- ✦ scratch paper
- ✦ poster paint
- ✦ paint brushes

Directions

1. Display a picture of *Mint, a Pretty Girl*. Ask students to pay particular attention to the details of Mint's garb. Observe her jewelry and the decorations attached to her dress. Try to identify the material of which each is made.

2. List a number of tribal names on the board (Mandan, Sioux, Cheyenne, Blackfeet, Crow, etc.). Have the students choose a tribe and research the clothing of that group.

3. Use the bags for canvas by cutting off the bottom.

4. Have each student tear the bag into a square or rectangular shape; then crumple it and smooth it out to simulate Catlin's portraits which he kept rolled in bundles.

5. On scratch paper, direct students to sketch a drawing of a Native American costume; when they are satisfied with the design, copy the designs onto the paper bags.

6. Color in the details with the paints.

44

Extensions

1. *George Catlin: Painter of the American West* (see listing below) is a fascinating account of one man's mission to document and record the Native American way of life. Before assigning students to read this biography, however, you may want to review it yourself. Descriptions of some of the Indian torture dances are particularly graphic and may be disturbing to the squeamish. As an alternate activity, you may want to choose some sections of the book to read aloud to the students.

2. Frederic Remington (1861-1909) was probably the most famous painter of the Wild West. Instruct the students to research this artist's life and write a list of ten facts they find out about him. As a class, make a chart comparing his life and art to that of George Catlin's.

3. In addition to painting Native American portraits, George Catlin also wrote some books about his expeditions. One of them was titled *My Life Amongst the Indians*. Tell students to stay in the mind of George Catlin as they write about one of the following:

    ✦ You have just witnessed a medicine man performing mysterious rites over a dying man. Write a letter home to your wife, Clara, describing the ceremony you have seen.

    ✦ During your travels you have collected Native American clothing, tepees, weapons, and other artifacts. In addition, you have painted 500 portraits and sketches of them. Draft a letter to the United States Senate asking them to buy your collection. In your letter, include your concerns about preserving the vanishing way of Native American life.

    ✦ To gather more information about the Native Americans you talk with trappers, traders, and fur company officials. Write a conversation you might have with one of these men about their knowledge of Native American ways.

4. George Catlin was a pioneer of American ethnography, that is, he studied specific cultures. In a class discussion have the students talk about the reasons they think Catlin's work is so important. Ask them to explain why his work met with praise, yet no one wanted to buy his whole collection. Find out when it was finally purchased and where it is now exhibited.

Recommended Reading _____

Artists of the Old West by John C. Ewers (Doubleday & Company, 1973)

George Catlin and the Old Frontier by Harold McCracken (Dial Press, 1979)

George Catlin: Painter of the Indian West by Mark Sufrin (Atheneum, 1991)

Edgar Degas

Edgar Degas was a man well known for his discontent. He often changed a completely finished painting by adding a touch of color. At times he would attach a strip of canvas on either side of an original surface vastly increasing its original size. Degas' restlessness can also be seen in the many phases his work encompassed and the variety of subject matter that interested him.

Perhaps Edgar's most favorite subject for his paintings was the ballerina. Since the public was forbidden to attend dance practices, he obtained a pass to the austere studios. For fifteen years he visited the institution and observed the ballerinas rehearsing. Degas used oils, pastels, and even created some sculptures to capture the unguarded moments in a ballerina's life. While he studied these dancers and painted them his whole career, he varied his point of observation and his techniques in each picture.

Another favorite subject for pictures was horse racing. Degas loved the pre-race excitement, the jockeys' colorful silks, and the anticipation of the horses before the upcoming race. Through his scenes of the race track the viewer is allowed to catch a glimpse of a particular moment in time that was of special interest to Edgar Degas.

While in Paris, Degas observed the people, the sights of the city, and the hustle and bustle of the busy art community. He spent many hours in the Opera House watching the musicians and listening to each of the instruments. Once when the orchestra caught his particular attention, he went into the musicians' pit. From this position he could barely see the stage where the ballerinas were dancing. The resulting picture of this event was *The Orchestra at the Opera*. It provided a whole new perspective for an artist to use in painting.

At the age of thirty-five, Edgar traveled to the United States with his brother, Rene, to visit their parents' cotton business in New Orleans, Louisiana. Here he patiently observed the workers which included his brothers, Rene and Achille. The resulting painting — *The Cotton Exchange, New Orleans* — was a huge success.

Later in his career, Degas experimented with a number of new techniques. In one he mixed pastels with liquid medium. He experimented with colored pencils and perfected a new system of engraving known as monotypes. Nearly blind by the age of 84, Edgar Degas died on September 27, 1917. This banker's son left the world with several glimpses of moments frozen in time.

Café—Concert at the Ambassadeurs

Focus: Degas employed the technique of foreshortening in which the distance between the foreground and the background of a picture is shortened.

Activity: Drawing a scene using the foreshortening technique

Vocabulary: foreshortening; monotype; perspective; Impressionist

Art Lesson

Materials

✦ art chalk, various colors
✦ liquid starch
✦ medium-point paintbrushes
✦ fingerpaint paper (or other paper with glossy surface)

Directions

1. Ask students to observe Degas' *Café—Concert at the Ambasssadeurs.* Find an example of foreshortening. Examine other paintings by Degas for the use of the foreshortening technique.

2. Have the students listen to the directions completely before they begin working on the project.

3. Use the rows of desks and chairs in the classroom as a model for the drawings. Talk about perspective from the particular viewing point of tne students and how they might foreshorten the foreground.

4. With the paintbrush, have students spread a layer of liquid starch over the entire surface of the paper. Students should work quickly to draw on the wet surface with the colored chalks. (If the paper becomes dry, spread more starch over the dry spots on the paper.)

5. Compare the completed projects. Determine which ones capture the foreshortening technique best.

Extensions

1. Degas became interested in photography, a new invention in the 1850s. Direct the students (or assign a group) to research the history of photography. Find out when it was invented and by whom. Have them describe a Kodak® box camera and explain how it worked.

2. Discuss with the students the effects that the invention of the camera had on the art world at that time. How might it have changed the point of view of the artist? What new types of painting might it have led to?

3. Degas liked to look for new and unusual points of view in his paintings. For example, rather than show a subject at eye level, he painted it so that the viewer had to look up or down at the subject. Look for examples of this technique in another artist's work.

4. In some of his paintings, Degas employed an asymmetrical arrangement. Talk about symmetry; look for some things in the classroom that are symmetrical. Discuss asymmetry and find some things that are asymmetrical. Observe Degas' painting, *The Star,* for its asymmetrical features. Group the students. Tell them to form a symmetrical pattern with their bodies; then have them form an asymmetrical pattern with their bodies.

5. Photographs often capture a subject unposed; these are called candid pictures. Tell the students to look through magazines to find samples of unposed pictures. Assign them to bring in a candid photo from their family albums, if possible.

6. Among Degas' friends were the painters Manet, Renoir, Monet, Pissarro, and Cassatt. Tell the students to find out more about these artists, their work, and details of their lives.

Recommended Reading

The Book of Art: Impressionism and Post-Impressionism, Vol. 7 edited by Alan Bowness (Grolier Incorporated, 1965)

Degas by Degas edited by Rachel Barnes (Alfred Knopf, 1990)

Famous People by Kenneth and Valerie McLeish (Troll Associates, 1991)

Meet Edgar Degas by Anne Newlands (J.B. Lippincott, 1988)

A Weekend with Degas by Rosabianca Skira-Venturi (Rizzoli International Publications, Inc., 1991)

Claude Monet

In France, during the 1800s, the only way for an artist to be recognized was to have his work accepted by the Salon. The judges, who usually favored traditional paintings, determined which art pieces would hang in the Salon and which would be rejected. When Claude Monet entered two paintings and both were rejected by the Salon, he never said another word to them. Years later, in dire need of money, he and a group of like-minded artists staged their own exhibition. At first, their work was met with derision and even anger, but by the late 1880s, Impressionism had become acceptable.

Oscar-Claude Monet (he later dropped Oscar) was born on November 14, 1840; he was the second son of Adolphe and Louise-Justine Monet. At school he would draw in the margins of all his schoolbooks and notebooks. By the age of 16, Claude was already famous as a caricature artist and commanded about 20 francs (about sixty dollars today) per portrait. When he was 18, he left for Paris where he studied at the Academie Suisse. War broke out in the spring of 1861, and Claude was drafted. After about two years of service, he returned to France to study art at a conventional studio.

One person who influenced Monet's style most was Eugene Boudoin who kept inviting Monet to join him in painting a landscape in the open air. To his amazement, Monet experienced colors and light as he had never seen them before. From then on the outdoors became his studio. Despite the weather conditions, Monet hauled his canvasses through fields, snow, and rain. Once he was swept underwater while painting an ocean scene.

During the 1860s and the 1870s, Monet and his family endured appalling poverty. At times he was forced to sell his possessions to have money for his paints. Many times Monet begged friends and family for loans. There were brief moments of hope, though, when someone would buy a painting or two. It was not until the late 1880s that their work became accepted.

Monet's art was distinct. One special effect was created when he applied small dabs of paint to the canvas and used color instead of black paint to represent shadows. This technique involved dabbing complementary colors, such as red and yellow, next to one another, allowing the viewer to see the resulting color orange. Another effect involved the variation in lighting conditions as the same subject was being painted. Monet would work on one canvas for only a few minutes before starting another. Then he would return to the same place day after day to wait for the return of that particular lighting effect. Despite some eyesight problems in his later years, Monet continued to paint until he died on December 5, 1926.

White and Yellow Water Lilies

Focus: Monet's goal in painting was to capture nature as he saw it in the moment.

Activity: Painting nature outdoors

Vocabulary: Impressionist; "optical mixing"; complementary

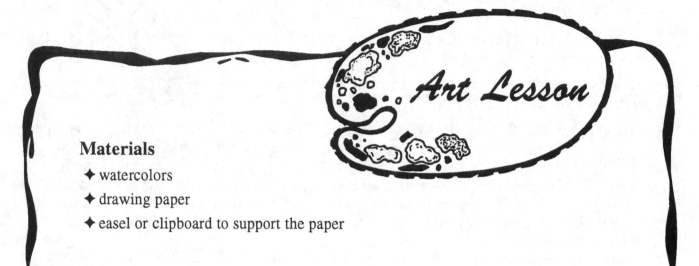

Art Lesson

Materials

✦ watercolors

✦ drawing paper

✦ easel or clipboard to support the paper

Directions

1. Direct the students' attention to the way the lilies fill the canvas and to the fact that there is no horizon line. Have them describe the colors and the tone of the painting.

2. Monet completed most of his paintings outdoors so it is fitting that students should simulate this same experience.

3. Attach the drawing paper to an easel or clipboard or some type of support.

4. Tell students to choose a subject and paint it just as they see it. Instruct them to remain in the same spot.

5. After about 10 to 15 minutes, have the students observe any changes in the lighting and paint another picture of the same subject.

6. If time permits and the students are interested, have them paint a third perspective of the same subject.

Extensions

1. The term Impressionism was inspired by Monet's painting *Impression Sunrise*. Display a picture of that painting and assign the following:

    ✦ Before learning the real story behind the term Impressionism, write a creative story explaining the origin of the term.

    ✦ Make a list of the painters who were in Monet's group; make a list of some later Impressionists.

2. Instead of using black to create a shadow effect, Monet made use of complementary colors. Have the students make a color wheel so they can readily identify complementary colors.

    Materials: white construction paper or card stock (available at copy shops); scissors; red, orange, yellow, green, blue, and violet crayons; compass

    Directions

    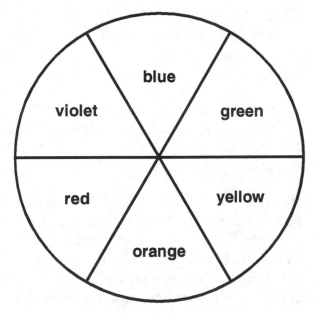

    ✦ With the compass, draw a circle on the construction paper or card stock; cut it out. Fold the circle in half so that the top half comes down to meet the bottom half.

    ✦ Grasp the two edges of the diameter and fold both sides inward until they meet in the center.

    ✦ Crease the fold lines; unfold to reveal a circle with six spaces.

    ✦ Color the top 3 spaces from left to right: violet, blue, green.

    ✦ Color the bottom 3 spaces from left to right: red, orange, yellow. Colors opposite on the wheel are complementary.

    ✦ **Follow-up:** Find out about Chevreul's Color Circle. Explain his "law of simultaneous contrast." A fine resource for this activity is *Eyewitness Art: Impressionism* (see listings below).

3. Learn more about Monet by reading *Linnea in Monet's Garden* or *The Natural World Through the Eyes of Artists* (see listings below). Create your own impressionist painting by dabbing colors onto a sheet of paper. Use a cotton swab instead of a paintbrush.

Recommended Reading _____

Claude Monet by Ann Waldron (Harry N. Abrams, 1991)

Eyewitness Art: Monet by Jude Welton (Dorling Kindersley, 1992)

Eyewitness Art: Impressionism by Jude Welton (Dorling Kindersley, 1993)

Linnea in Monet's Garden by Christina Bjork and Lena Anderson (R&S Books, 1985)

Monet by Monet by Claude Monet (Alfred A. Knopf, 1990)

The Natural World Through the Eyes of Artists by Wendy and Jack Richardson (Children's Press, 1991)

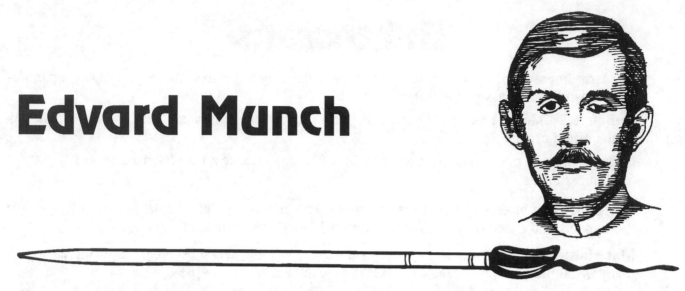

Edvard Munch

Edvard Munch is considered his country's greatest artist. He was a forerunner of Expressionism and an inspiration for the German Expressionist movement. An outsider, a brooder, and a melancholy person, Edvard called his paintings his "children." He felt he had no one else. Surely his traumatic childhood contributed to these intense feelings.

When he was just five years old, Edvard's mother died. Nine years later his sister also died. Edvard's father was so affected by his wife's death that he suffered from religious mania to insane violence. As a child, Edvard himself was rather sickly. It is no surprise, then, that death and sickness are a constant theme in much of his work.

At the age of seventeen Munch entered the Oslo School of Art and Handicraft. During his time there, he was influenced by realist painter Christian Krog. Munch, however, was developing a style that was unlike any of his Norwegian contemporaries. By the late 1880s, Norway became aware of the French Impressionists. Edvard visited Paris for a few weeks in 1885 and later won a scholarship to a school there. Radical changes took place in his style. In 1892, he was invited to exhibit in Berlin. His work caused such public outcry that the show was closed. It went on, however, to Munich and other German cities and Copenhagen.

Four years later in 1896, Edvard was in Paris again, this time to concentrate on working with woodcuts. He was able to make some technical innovations in this art form by employing a new method of cutting up the blocks. In addition, he allowed the grain of the wood to help dictate its form.

By the early twentieth century Munch had been professionally recognized in Norway and had achieved financial security. His personal life continued to erode. Edvard entered a sanitorium to recover. While there, he was able to continue his work; he even entered a competition.

Throughout his life, Edvard worked in spurts. For months at a time he would not paint a thing, and then he would begin to work in a frenzy. His specialty was in portraying extreme emotions such as jealousy and loneliness. He purposely tried to evoke strong emotions in his viewer. In his last years' works, he seemed to sum up his life experiences and became obsessed with his youth and the irony of old age.

Edvard Munch was born on December 12, 1863, and died in 1944. His work was very influential in the development of modern art.

The Scream

Focus: A painting should evoke strong emotions in its viewers.

Activity: Painting a picture that portrays strong emotion

Vocabulary: Expressionism; modern art

Art Lesson

Materials

✦ colored crayons or marking pens

✦ white construction paper or drawing paper

Directions

1. *The Scream* is Edvard Munch's most famous work. Ask students to describe the emotions the subject of the painting might be feeling. Talk about how the painting affects their own feelings.

2. Tell the students to think about a time when they had a strong feeling of joy or jealousy or fear (or any other emotion).

3. Using crayons or marking pens have them draw a picture of that event. Encourage the use of color to express emotion and distorted figures to convey their feelings.

4. Repeat this procedure using neon-colored crayons and markers. Compare the two completed pictures. Which one has more visual impact?

5. Extend the project by having students write about their drawings, if they would like.

Extensions

1. Munch's painting, *The Scream,* is his most famous. It represents the fear of losing one's mind.

   ✦ What events in Munch's life might have contributed to his own fear of losing his mind?

   ✦ Through the years this painting has come to represent high anxiety. Direct the students to draw a picture of someone who is extremely anxious and afraid.

   ✦ Discuss with students their biggest fear (heights, snakes, etc.). Ask them to draw a picture of themselves confronting their fears.

2. Locate Norway on a map or globe. Divide the class into groups and have them complete a report on Norway. Each group will need a file folder, a pair of scissors, and some markers.

   ✦ Draw the outline of Norway onto a file folder, making one edge of the country as close to the fold as possible.

   ✦ Cut out around the country's shape except for the fold.

   ✦ On the outside of the shape, label Munch's birthplace of Loyten with his date of birth and death. Mark and label Oslo with the Oslo School of Art and Handicraft.

   ✦ Inside the Norway shape students should write a brief report about Munch. Include facts about his childhood, schooling, and art works.

   ✦ On the back cover include a drawing of Munch's *The Scream.*

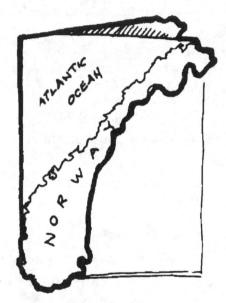

3. An 1892 exhibition of Munch's works in Berlin had to be closed because the paintings were considered to be shocking. Ask the students to explain why they think his art was shocking to the people. Tell them to keep in mind the other artists of the day and their works. With the students, discuss how Munch's works might be received today if he were showing them for the very first time.

4. Edvard Munch was influenced by the art work of Vincent van Gogh. Have the students discuss some things that they think the two artists had in common in their personal lives as well as their professional lives.

Recommended Reading _____

The Annotated Mona Lisa by Carol Strickland, Ph.D., and John Boswell (Andrews and McMeel, 1992)

The Book of Art: Impressionists and Post-Impressionists, Vol. 7., edited by Alan Bowness (Grolier Incorporated, 1965)

Understanding Modern Art by Monica Bohm-Duchen and Janet Cook (EDC Publishing, 1988)

Henri Rousseau

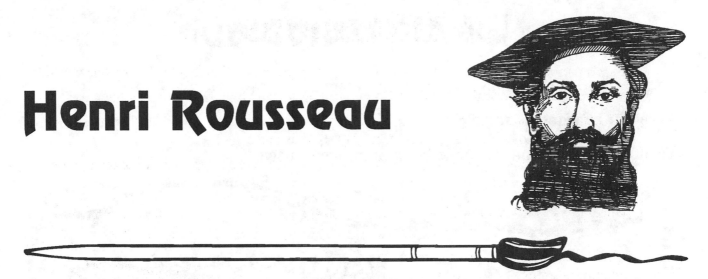

Henri Rousseau is considered the first and greatest of the primitive (or naïve) painters. His style of painting is called primitive because he had no formal training in art. In fact, he had very little formal education in general. Friends and acquaintances considered him to be dull and rather naïve.

Henri was born in 1844 in Laval, France, a small city in the northern part of that country. His father was a tinsmith. When Henri was eighteen years old, he was drafted into the military where he was a musician in their band. Four years later, he was released and went to work as a clerk. Because he worked in the Paris customs service for several years, he was nicknamed the Douanier or Customs Official, although he never actually achieved that high a ranking. During his spare time, Rousseau took up painting as a hobby. As he progressed in his artistic abilities, he became so confident of his talents that he retired from his customs service job at the age of forty. This enabled Henri to collect a small pension and devote himself to art full time. To supplement his income, he taught drawing and the violin. He also found time to spend with his wife, Clemence, and even write poems, plays, and music.

This French Grandma Moses is best known for his jungle scenes. Ironically, the only jungles he ever saw were in books. He visited the local zoo and botanical gardens from which he gathered ideas which he embellished with his own vivid imagination. Rousseau also sang loudly while he worked to keep up his spirits. For his habit of singing while painting and for his art work, he suffered much ridicule.

In 1906, Henri met artist Pablo Picasso who was greatly influenced by the work of his new-found acquaintance. Picasso considered Rousseau to be a truly original artist, but many of Rousseau's own colleagues enjoyed playing practical jokes on him. Once, Picasso hosted a party for his new friend. Unfortunately, it was half serious and half in jest, but Henri did not seem to notice the insults. He took everything as a compliment and even wrote Picasso a thank-you note for the festivities.

A year after Rousseau began painting fulltime, he was already exhibiting at the Salon des Independents. For the most part, though, the public did not react favorably to his work ,and he lived in poverty. Parisian artists recognized and lauded his abilities, even if they did consider him to be somewhat dense. When told that his work was as beautiful as Giotto's, Rousseau asked, "Who's Giotto?" Had he had any formal art training, he would have been familiar with the great Renaissance painter. Rousseau died on September 4, 1910, and was buried in a pauper's grave.

Exotic Landscape

Focus: Base your paintings on your imagination.

Activity: Drawing a jungle plant

Vocabulary: Surrealism; modern art; primitive or naïve

Art Lesson

Materials

- ✦ pencils
- ✦ art chalk
- ✦ cotton swabs
- ✦ newspaper
- ✦ fixative or hair spray
- ✦ 9" x 12" (23 cm x 30 cm) black construction paper
- ✦ liquid white glue in dispensers

Directions

1. Observe the painting and notice the details Rousseau used. Ask the students to describe some of the details and possibly name some of the jungle plants.

2. Instruct the students to choose a jungle plant for their drawing.

3. Direct them to use the pencil to draw one plant on the whole surface of the paper.

4. Go over the pencil lines with the white glue; allow to dry overnight.

5. Spread newspaper over the working surface before filling in the plant with the colored chalk.

6. Blend the chalk with the cotton swab or a finger.

7. Carefully shake off excess chalk over newspaper. Take the finished painting outside and spray with art fixative or hair spray to set the chalk.

Extensions

1. Henri Rousseau was considered the forerunner of the Surrealists. Establish that the Surrealist movement produced art which was based on the thoughts and feelings of the unconscious and subconscious mind.

    ✦ Observe some of Rousseau's work. Ask students what they think the artist was trying to say in each painting or have them write a creative story or poem about one of the pictures.

    ✦ Marc Chagall, Salvador Dali, and Paul Klee were also Surrealists. Divide the students into three groups and assign each group one of these three artists. Tell the students to compare their assigned artist with Henri Rousseau. Explain how the two artists' work is alike and different and make a list of ways in which the two artists were alike and different in their characteristics.

2. Rousseau liked to sing while he was painting. Ask students to name some songs they might like to sing while they paint. After agreeing on one song, direct the students to softly sing it as they draw a picture. After completing the drawings, discuss the experiment. Was it difficult or easy to sing and paint? Did they enjoy doing the two simultaneously or did they find it to be distracting?

3. One unique characteristic of Rousseau's paintings is the glossy finish of the surfaces. He achieved this by polishing the completed picture. Have the students create a glossy picture with this project. Each student will need crayons, tagboard or white card stock (available at copy stores), and newspaper.

    ✦ Spread newspaper across the working surface.

    ✦ With the crayons draw a design over the whole surface of the tagboard or card stock.

    ✦ Fill in the spaces with heavy layers of color by pressing down hard on the crayons. This should create a glossy look.

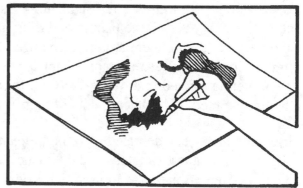

4. Display a picture of Rousseau's *The Sleeping Gypsy.* Discuss with the students the feelings this picture evokes in them. Do words like mysterious, eerie, or haunting describe it? What other words can they think of to describe this work?

Recommended Reading _____

The Book of Art: Impressionists and Post-Impressionists, Vol. 7, edited by Alan Bowness (Grolier Incorporated, 1965)

Famous Artists of the Past by Alice Elizabeth Chase (Platt & Munk, 1964)

Henri Rousseau by Ernest Raboff (Harper & Row, 1988)

Start Exploring: Masterpieces by Mary Martin (Running Press, 1990) (This book includes 60 masterpieces to color.)

Georges Seurat

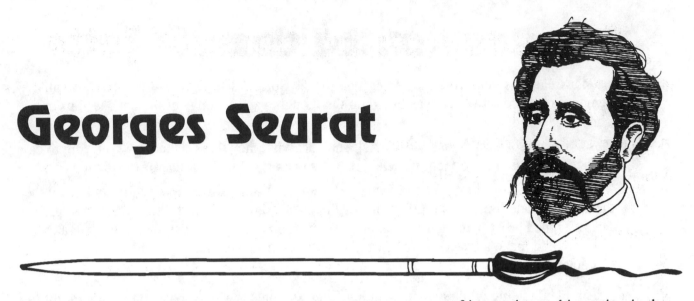

Throughout the nineteenth century, there was an enormous amount of innovation and invention in the fields of science and art. The Impressionist artists such as Claude Monet experimented with light in art. Scientists, too, were interested in light and they sought to explain how we see colors. Color theories of scientist Chevreul caught Georges Seurat's attention, and he put these theories to work in his paintings. Seurat found that if he placed unmixed colors side by side on the canvas rather than mixing them first on the palette, the effect was a greater vibrancy of color. In addition , his new technique consisted of painting with small dots of color rather than long strokes. The term pointillism was used to describe this technique.

Because this art form required such an intense amount of time and work, Georges was only able to complete only seven large paintings during his ten-year career. He planned each painting with care and patience giving them a more formalized look than the sense of the moment captured by the Impressionists. It was the Impressionists who first influenced Seurat's work. He admired their use of color, yet he wanted to develop a system for achieving their color effects. Gradually Seurat devised the unique method of placing dots of unmixed colors onto the canvas.

Probably his most celebrated work is *A Sunday on La Grande Jatte*. Its finished size is 207 cm tall by 308 cm wide (approximately 6 feet 8 inches by 10 feet), and it took him two years to complete. This painting even inspired the Broadway musical, *Sunday in the Park with George* by Stephen Sondheim.

Georges Seurat came from a comfortable background so he never had to worry about making money while he was pursuing his artistic endeavors. Military service in 1879 interrupted his studies at the Ecole des Beaux Arts in Paris. Upon completion of his military duty, he returned to drawing. It was during this time that he developed pointillism.

This talented artist died suddenly in 1891 at the age of 31, possibly from meningitis. He was survived by his mistress and a son. Artist Edgar Degas had nicknamed him "the notary" because of his top hat and dark suit with its precisely pressed pants. His art reflected this meticulous appearance. Although Seurat's style did not last many years, his art is still greatly admired and respected even today.

58

A Sunday on La Grande Jatte

Focus: Colors can best be portrayed through dots of unmixed color placed side by side on the canvas.

Activity: Creating a picture with dots

Vocabulary: Neo-Impressionism; pointillism

Art Lesson

Materials

+ one-hole punch
+ colored construction paper
+ tagboard or other heavy paper
+ glue stick
+ tempera or poster paints
+ paintbrushes

Directions

1. Have the students observe a television picture up close and then from farther away. Are they able to see the dots which compose an image? Observe one of Seurat's paintings; notice the dot technique.

2. Students can create their own dotted pictures with the following art activity.

   + Direct students to make a number of construction paper dots with the hole punch.

   + Glue the dots to the tagboard background to create an image, such as a flowerpot, an animal, or food. Remind the students to keep the dots close together to resemble pointillism.

   + Add dots of complementary paint to give the picture added depth.

   + Display the finished products and observe them from afar.

Extensions

1. Georges Seurat is credited with founding Neo-Impressionism. This movement is based on scientific principles which resulted in formalized composition.

   ✦ Have some students research the Neo-Impressionist movement and find out the names of some other artists who practiced that type of art.

   ✦ Neo-Impressionism was just one of the "ism" movements in art in the nineteenth century. Assign the students to research and find out more about any of the following: Impressionism, Post-Impressionism, Expressionism, or Symbolism.

2. Review the concepts of primary colors and complementary colors. Some background information on this topic can be found in *Painting* (An Usborne Book) by Patience Foster (Usborne Publishing, 1981).

3. Assign a group of students to find out more about the scientist Chevreul and his theories of how we see color. Have them report their findings to the rest of the class. An excellent resource for this project is *Impressionism* by Jude Welton (Dorling Kindersley, 1993).

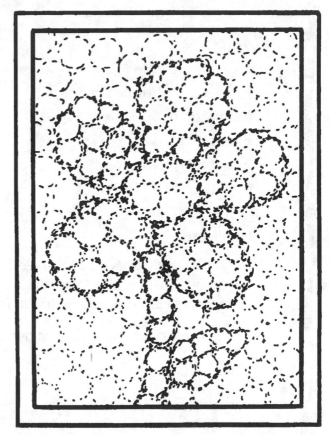

4. *Pointillism* gives finished pictures a look of graininess, even when they are viewed from afar. Let the students make "grainy" pictures. Each one will need a piece of sandpaper and some colored chalks. Instruct the students to draw a design directly onto the sandpaper with the chalk.

5. Learn more about Seurat's techniques by reading page 45 in *The Story in a Picture: Children in Art* by Robin Richmond (see listing below). The text explains Chevreul's rule and also helps the reader understand Seurat's 1884 painting, *Bathers*.

Recommended Reading _____

Great Painters by Piero Ventura (G.P. Putnam's Sons, 1984)

The Story in a Picture: Children in Art by Robin Richmond (Ideals Children's Books, 1992)

Vincent van Gogh

During his lifetime he sold only one painting; he died a poor man. It is ironic, therefore, that more than a hundred years after his death, his painting, *Portrait of Dr. Gachet,* was purchased for $82.5 million dollars. This was the most expensive painting ever sold. The story of van Gogh's life is filled with other amazing facts and events.

Vincent Willem van Gogh was born in the village of Groot Zundert on March 30, 1853. Van Gogh was the eldest of six children. His father, Theodorus van Gogh, was a preacher; his mother, Anna Carbentus, supported her son's artistic talents. Vincent attended the local village school and went on to boarding school at the age of twelve. There he developed his lifelong love of literature. When he was 16, he joined his uncle's art firm in Hague. Four years later, he was transferred to London, England. He enjoyed his work, but life there was marred by an unfortunate incident. Vincent had fallen in love with his landlady's daughter, and he took her rejection particularly hard. He became sullen and withdrawn. His uncle, hoping that a change of scenery would do him some good, arranged for Vincent to be transferred to Paris, but after only three months, he was dismissed. By 1876, van Gogh had returned to Holland. Driven by a need to spread the Gospel to the poor, he moved to a poor coal-mining district, gave away all his possessions, and ministered to the sick. Throughout this period, van Gogh continued his drawings and eventually realized that he could serve God better through his art work.

In 1886, van Gogh moved to Paris to live with his brother Theo, an art dealer. Vincent's style changed rapidly there as he studied the works of Pissarro, Monet, and other Impressionists. From Paris he moved into a yellow house in Arles. Van Gogh intended for it to be a studio and center for painters, but only artist Paul Gauguin came. This was a disastrous arrangement as the two quarreled about everything. One day after a particularly violent argument with Gauguin, Vincent cut off part of his own ear. The next year, he finally agreed to enter the asylum of Saint-Remy where he could continue his art while he recovered. A recovery never came about. Vincent continued to suffer from attacks of mental breakdown interspersed with lucid, rational periods. Realizing that he would never be free of this illness and feeling like a burden on his brother Theo, Vincent shot himself to death on July 27, 1890. An unknown when he died, there is now a state museum dedicated to van Gogh in Amsterdam. Vincent van Gogh is probably the most reproduced painter in history.

The Yellow House

Focus: Van Gogh painted everyday, familiar things.

Activity: Painting a house

Vocabulary: Post-Impressionist; impasto

Art Lesson

Materials

- ✦ cornstarch
- ✦ plastic spoons
- ✦ plastic lids for palettes
- ✦ tempera paints
- ✦ wood craft sticks or plastic knives
- ✦ cardboard (from a cereal box or other container)

Directions

1. Draw students' attention to van Gogh's use of color in *The Yellow House* and other works. With the class make a list of some of the other characteristics of a typical van Gogh painting.

2. Explain to students that in this assignment, they will create colorful pictures of their houses, real or imagined. They will use the impasto style van Gogh used.

3. Using a plastic lid as a palette, have the students mix some cornstarch into a tempera color with the spoon.

4. Apply the color to the cardboard surface with a craft stick or plastic knife to imitate the impasto style.

5. Continue to mix other colors in the same manner and apply to the cardboard "canvas." Encourage the students to use lots of color.

Extensions

1. Van Gogh's middle brother, Theo, remained his most staunch supporter over the years. He supplied Vincent with money and a place to stay just so he could continue his art work. Throughout his lifetime, Vincent wrote over 700 letters to Theo in which he described his paintings and his attitudes toward life.

   ✦ Pretend you are Vincent van Gogh and you have just finished painting *The Yellow House*. In a letter to Theo describe your feelings about life. Keep in mind that your dream at this point is to create a center for painters.

   ✦ Pretend you are van Gogh and you have just argued with artist Paul Gaugin about technique. Gauguin insists that it is better to paint from memory while you prefer to paint what you see. Write a conversation the two artists might have had over this point.

2. Show the class a picture of van Gogh's *Postman Roulin*. Have students create a mixed media portrait using a decorative background. Provide scraps of wallpaper, 12" x 18" (30 cm x 46 cm) sheets of drawing paper, and construction paper (Choose surplus colors, as they will not show on final portrait.), glue, and scissors.

   ✦ Ask students to draw a portrait of a family member or a friend. (The Roulins were friends of Van Gogh's and he painted several members of their family.) Have students color or paint the portrait, allow it to dry, and cut out the portrait. Students can choose a scrap of decorative wallpaper for the background. Glue this onto the construction paper so that it covers at least the top two-thirds of the paper. Glue the portrait to the foreground.

3. Assign students to find out the difference between Impressionists and Post-Impressionists. Make a class chart of the two groups.

4. If available, rent the video of *Lust for Life* to show the students as an introduction to Vincent van Gogh. (Preview the film yourself to determine its suitability for your class.)

Recommended Reading _____

Eyewitness Art: Van Gogh by Bruce Bernard (Dorling Kindersley, 1992)

Lives of the Artists by M.B. Goffstein (Farrar, Straus and Giroux, 1981)

Looking for Vincent by Thea Dubelaar (Checkerboard Press, 1990)

The Self-Portrait in Art by Sharon Lerner (Lerner Publications, 1965)

Van Gogh by Mike Venezia (Children's Press, 1988)

Van Gogh and His World by Terry Measham (Silver Burdett Press, 1990)

Van Gogh by Van Gogh edited by Rachel Barnes (Alfred Knopf, 1990)

Twentieth Century Artists

While the nineteenth century saw its share of strife and change within the art world, the era that followed brought with it even more evolution. Art became less concerned with visual reality than with the artist's inner vision. Anything and everything was considered a suitable subject for art; no longer were artists limited to portraits or nature pictures. Traditional rules about color were erased; colors did not have to accurately represent the object. Skies could be red or blue or green to reflect the emotions and feelings of the artist. Any number of materials were at an artist's disposal to use in creating art. Freedom of expression was the most important concern now that there was no need to please a private patron, as was the style in earlier times. Gradually, art moved toward pure abstraction in which form, line, and color were the rule.

Although the School of Paris dominated the first half of the century with its Fauvist, Cubist, and Surrealist movements, the United States took over the spotlight in the 1950s with the advent of Abstract Expressionism. In this genre, also known as action painting, energy and action are stressed.

The technique in Abstract Impressionism includes the free application of paint in which the creative process is more important than the end product. Today, no one movement dominates the art world. Instead, art is recognized as a means to express oneself through any medium, through any subject.

Twentieth Century Artists (cont.)

Below is a listing of the artists represented in this section. Following each name and country of origin is a brief statement indicating particularly noteworthy achievements.

Artist	Country	Achievements
Marc Chagall (1887-1985)	Russia	known for imaginative fantasies (forerunner of the Surrealist movement)
Frida Kahlo (1907-1954)	Mexico	created fantasy-like self-portraits on topics of marriage and childbirth
Paul Klee (1879-1940)	Switzerland	used color and line and deceptively simple artwork
Jacob Lawrence (1917-)	U.S.A.	told the history of African Americans through his art
Henri Matisse (1869-1954)	France	used color to create art that rebelled against realism; popularized collage
Piet Mondrian (1872-1944)	Holland	self-proclaimed purpose was to eliminate emotion from art
Grandma Moses (1860-1961)	U.S.A.	began career as primitive artist at age of 70
Louise Nevelson (1900-1988)	Russia/U.S.A.	pioneered environmental sculpture; noted for her walls of cubical pieces of wood
Georgia O'Keefe (1887-1986)	U.S.A.	best known for her magnified irises and calla lilies as well as her desert landscapes Mexico
Pablo Picasso (1881-1973)	Spain	one of the inventors of Cubism, the major art revolution of the twentieth century
Horace Pippin (1888-1946)	U.S.A.	talented primitive artist who did not begin his art career until he was in his forties
Tammy Rahr (1958-)	U.S.A.	creates toys representing Native American culture
Faith Ringgold (1930-)	U.S.A.	demonstrates her African-American heritage through watercolors, masks, and quilts
Charlene Teters (1952-)	U.S.A.	native American painter who incorporates objects with her art
Wang Yani (1975-)	China	called the Picasso of China; has already produced over ten thousand paintings

Marc Chagall

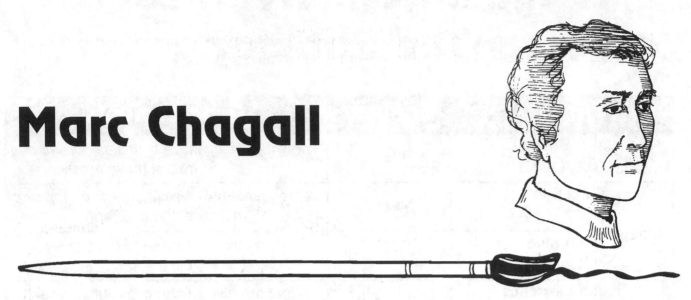

Marc Chagall was born on July 7, 1887, in a small Russian village. He was the first son born to Zahar and Feiga-Ita Chagall. Zahar was a worker in a herring packing house. Mrs. Chagall raised their nine children and also had a small grocery store in her home to supplement the family income.

When Marc first announced his plans to become an artist, his mother was shocked. (The Chagalls were a Jewish family who believed that it was a sin to make images.) An uncle in the family finally convinced everyone to at least let the boy try. Marc entered Yehuda Pen's art school, but soon found that his interpretation of art was very different from what was being taught. He would have to go to Petersburg to learn his craft.

At that time in history, the Jews were treated harshly and had to receive special permission to stay in the city. Through a family friend, Marc was able to obtain a permit. An art academy accepted him and even offered him a small scholarship. As his own style emerged, he knew he would have to move on to Paris. Unfortunately, Chagall's paintings did not sell well since he followed no particular school of painting, nor did his work fall into any currently fashionable classification.

In 1914, a German poet and art dealer arranged to exhibit three of Marc's paintings and later scheduled a one-man show. The public response was warm and enthusiastic. The day after the exhibit's opening, Chagall traveled to Russia to visit his family. Before he could leave Vitebsk, the Germans declared war on Russia and all travel was halted. Trapped, Chagall turned to his art work and in the ensuing year completed nearly 60 paintings and drawings. While there, he also married his long-time fiancee´, Bella.

Through the years, Chagall worked on some important projects. He was responsible for establishing an academy of arts in Vitebsk. In Moscow he designed the sets and costumes for the newly-opened State Jewish Theatre. He completed a series of etchings for *Dead Souls,* one of the greatest novels of the nineteenth century. Vollard, a book publisher, hired Marc to do etchings for two books, including the *Bible.*

When World War II erupted and France surrendered to Germany, it was no longer safe for Jews. Chagall, his wife Bella, and daughter Ida emigrated to the United States. Unfortunately, his beloved Bella died during their stay in New York City. When it was safe, Chagall and his daughter returned to Paris where he continued to work until he died on March 28, 1985, at the age of 97.

66

The Birthday

Focus: Chagall told stories with his paintings.

Activity: Painting a fantasy story

Vocabulary: Cubist; pastel; fantasy

Art Lesson

Materials

✦ scissors

✦ wooden craft stick or butter knife

✦ sprinkles and other cake decorations

✦ cardboard from cereal boxes or shoe boxes

✦ canned frosting (or make your own with powdered sugar and water)

Directions

1. Establish that Marc Chagall is telling how he feels about his birthday in this painting. Based on the colors and images in *The Birthday,* have students describe what they think the artist is saying. (For a complete description see *Marc Chagall* by Ernest Raboff, Harper & Row, 1988.)

2. Tell the students that they are going to make a fantasy birthday cake.

3. With the scissors, cut out any type of shape from the cardboard.

4. Spread a layer of frosting on the cake, using the craft stick or knife.

5. Decorate the cake with sprinkles, cake decorations, or torn bits of paper or paper dots. Let dry.

6. **Alternate activity:** Let students decorate real cupcakes or a sheet cake.

Extensions

1. Extend the lesson on page 67 with this activity. Tell students that Chagall used bold colors and distortion to convey his feelings. In *The Birthday,* he communicates his love for his fianceé through the use of warm, bright colors and their movement — they look as if they are floating in mid-air.

   ✦ Ask the students to think of some metaphors used to describe being in love (e.g., head over heels; on cloud nine; etc.). Which one of these best describes Chagall's painting?

   ✦ Brainstorm more expressions and record them. (For a complete list see *101 American English Idioms* by Harry Collis, Passport Books, 1989). Ask students to draw literal interpretations of four of them.

2. Marc Chagall often could not afford canvases for his art work so he used bed sheets, tablecloths, and even his shirts. Have the students bring in an old tee shirt to paint on. Or, provide a tablecloth or sheet for each group of students and have them paint a mural modeled after Marc Chagall's style.

3. When Marc told his mother that he wanted to be a painter, she was so shocked that she almost dropped the pan of bread she was putting into the oven. Mrs. Chagall told her son that Jewish boys did not become painters, that he would never be able to make a living as a painter, and that she was concerned about what their friends might say.

   ✦ You are Marc. How would you counter each argument? Write a conversation you might have had with your mother; address each of her three concerns.

4. Display a number of Marc Chagall's paintings. With the class, brainstorm words that describe his art (dreamlike, joyous, bright, colorful, etc.). Record the words and direct the students to write a paragraph about Chagall, using as many of those words as possible.

5. Avant-garde is a French term which is applied to artists who defy the establishment. Could Marc Chagall be described as avant-garde? Ask the students to defend their answers.

Recommended Reading _____

Marc Chagall by Howard Greenfeld (Harry N. Abrams, Inc., 1989)

Marc Chagall by Ernest Raboff (Harper & Row, 1988)

Marc Chagall: Painter of Dreams by Natalie S. Bober (The Jewish Publication Society, 1991)

Frida Kahlo

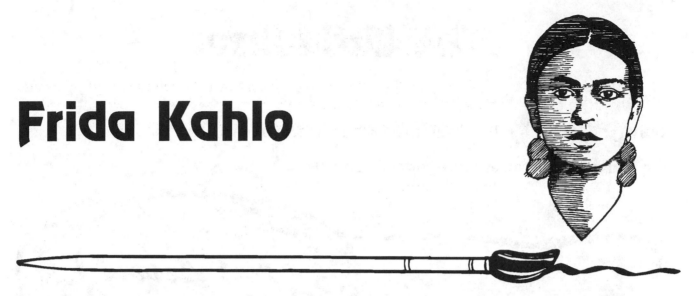

Frida Kahlo was born on July 6, 1907, in Coyoacan, Mexico, a small town near Mexico City. Her father, Guillermo, was a professional photographer and an amateur painter. He taught Frida about all the wonderful things in nature such as rocks, birds, insects, animals, and shells. In addition, he gave her lessons in photography and Mexican archaeology and art. From her mother, Matilde, Frida learned how to cook, sew, embroider, and keep a clean house.

When she was six years old, Frida contracted polio and was bedridden for nine months. During this time, she created an imaginary friend to help her through this lonely period in her life. With the encouragement of her father, Frida began to swim, skate, bicycle, and play ball to help strengthen her right leg which remained shorter than the other one. Some of her playmates made fun of her and called her "peg leg."

At age 15, Frida entered prep school where she planned to study to become a doctor. A tragic accident a few years later changed her life dramatically. When a trolley car hit her school bus, she was thrown into the street. Her injuries included broken ribs, spine, and collarbone. The most serious injury occurred when a steel handrail pierced her stomach. Frida was not expected to survive, but she was determined to live. Recovery was slow, and she was required to stay in bed. The doctor ordered her to wear a brace, and she was not allowed to sit up. Frida's mother had a special easel built so that she could paint from her prone position.

After her recuperation, Frida took her finished paintings to Diego Rivera, a famous Mexican artist. Diego not only encouraged her in her work, but he eventually married her. She began to take art more seriously and painted pictures that reflected her Mexican heritage. Still, her paintings reflected her sadness. Frida never fully recovered from the accident despite the many operations performed to straighten her spine and repair her foot. Often, she was in pain. Diego, her husband, did not always treat her well. In addition, she could not have children, a circumstance which saddened her most of all. These experiences and feelings were expressed in her paintings.

In her forties, Frida's health gradually failed. She died at the age of 47 on July 13, 1954. About a year before her death, however, she put on a major exhibit of her work. Her four-poster bed was moved into the art gallery and decorated with papier-mâché skeletons and photos of Diego and some of her political heroes. At the show's opening she wore a beautiful Mexican gown and was placed on the bed. Despite her ill health, she was determined to go out with a flourish. Today her paintings live on to tell the story of the tragedies and joys in her life.

The Little Deer

Focus: Frida Kahlo used art to fight life's obstacles.

Activity: Creating a self-portrait to depict a problem or challenge

Vocabulary: Mexican art; self-portrait; surrealist

Art Lesson

Materials

- ✦ drawing paper or construction paper
- ✦ scissors
- ✦ glue stick or white household glue
- ✦ old magazines
- ✦ pencils
- ✦ colored pencils or markers

Directions

1. Look closely at the picture *The Little Deer.* Tell the students to explain what the arrows in the deer's body might represent. Discuss the significance of the broken branch and the forest setting.

2. Direct the students to think of problems which they have had to overcome or to think of situations in their lives which have made them sad, angry, or disappointed.

3. Have the students look through the magazines and find a picture of an animal that best suits this feeling. Ask them to cut out the picture and glue it onto the drawing or construction paper.

4. Encourage students to draw an appropriate background scene and add any desired details they to the animal.

Extensions

1. As a follow-up to the art lesson on the page 70, direct the students to write a story about the picture they have created. Share the stories in small groups.

2. If possible, examine the art book, *Frida Kahlo Folding Screen* (Chronicle Books, 1992). There is no text — the pages unfold into one, long continuous screen of some of her paintings. Instruct the students to make their own folding book. Have them cut a sheet of 9" x 12" (23 cm x 30 cm) construction paper in half along the length (make a "hot dog" fold) and then tape the two 4.5" x 12" (11.5 cm x 30 cm) sections together. Accordion fold the resulting piece. In each section, have the students write the name of one of Frida's paintings and a written description of it. Tell them to draw a sketch of each painting to accompany the text. Display the finished projects on a special table.

3. Discuss how Frida's health may have affected her art. How might her art have been different if she had never been hurt in the accident? How might her art had been different if she and her husband Diego had been happier together or had been able to have children?

4. Observe a number of Kahlo's paintings. What examples of her Mexican heritage can be seen in her pictures? Direct the students to draw pictures that reflect their own ethnic origins (or any ethnic origin they may choose).

5. Frida's husband was Diego Rivera, a well-known artist in his own right. Assign a group of students to research Rivera's art and his family background by reading *Diego Rivera* by James Cockcroft (Chelsea House, 1991). Have them report their findings to the rest of the class. What other husband-wife art teams can they find out about?

6. Frida had many pets and liked to think of herself as an animal. Ask the students what they would be and why if they could be any animal in the world. Tell them to draw a picture of themselves as that animal and write an accompanying story about an adventure they might have.

Recommended Reading _____

Diego Rivera by James Cockcroft (Chelsea House, 1991)

Frida Kahlo: An Open Life by Raquel Tibol (University of New Mexico, 1993)

Frida Kahlo Folding Screen (Chronicle Books, 1992)

Inspirations: Stories About Women Artists by Leslie Sills (Albert Whitman and Company, 1988)

The Story in a Picture: Children in Art by Robin Richmond (Ideals Children's Books, 1992)

Paul Klee

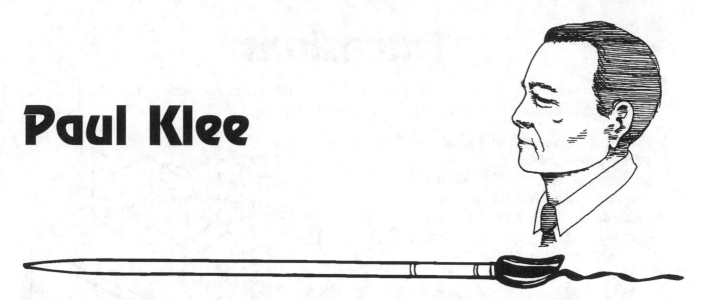

Paul Klee was born in Bern, Switzerland, on December 18, 1879. His father, Hans, was a music teacher and his mother, Ida, was a singer and an amateur painter. As a child Paul drew constantly. Cats were a favorite subject of his. Then at the age of seven, he learned to play the violin, which he continued throughout his adult life. In fact, he even played with the Berlin Municipal Orchestra for a time. Although music was important to Paul, he decided to become an artist.

Klee was a good student; he mastered several languages, histories, and sciences. In 1898, he began his art career by studying at the Munich Academy. After a few years, he traveled to Italy and then back to Munich. It was there that he made his first etchings and had his first one-man show which consisted of prints only. Later, he was invited to join the staff of the Bauhaus where he taught painting. Paul also kept a notebook of his artistic insights and ideas and published a number of books about art.

Unlike some of his fellow artists, Klee's work was more intuitive than scientific. Wassily Kandinsky, for example, sought to explain his development in a systematic way; Piet Mondrian planned his work out with mathematical precision. Paul Klee, however, knew he wanted his viewers to feel something when they looked at one of his paintings. In his abstract style, objects looked different from the way they appeared in real life. He loved color, and he liked to use numbers and letters as symbols in his works. Sometimes he just painted shapes and colors. In all of his work, he changed the natural look of things and gave his pictures a feeling of energy, movement, and rhythm. This movement and rhythm reflected his musical talents.

Through the years Klee's style changed as he tried new ideas. He experimented with a number of painting surfaces and mediums. At times, he painted on rough cloth with one kind of paint only to cover it with another type of paint. Chalks, paste, and crayons were applied to give colors a special glow. Pen and ink was another medium he explored. As Klee grew older, he painted with darker colors and the titles of his works became more serious. Throughout this change, however, Paul Klee's works still reflected his sense of humor and fantasy.

When Paul Klee died at the age of sixty in 1940, he had created an impressive amount of work: over ten thousand drawings and nearly five thousand paintings during his lifetime. This most prolific artist brought humor to the absurdities of life and a feeling of light-hearted affection to all that he drew.

The Niesen

Focus: Klee expressed his outlook on life through lines and color.

Activity: Drawing an imaginary picture using lines and color

Vocabulary: abstract; geometric; distortion

Art Lesson

Materials

- ✦ graph paper with one-inch squares
- ✦ watercolors or colored pencils
- ✦ thin-line black marking pen

Directions

1. *The Niesen* was painted by Klee after an expedition to North Africa in 1914. Have the students identify the pyramid in the background. Note the multicolored building blocks in the foreground. What other details can the students discern?

2. Direct the students to fold the graph paper in half from top to bottom; unfold.

3. Establish that the top portion is the background and the lower section is the foreground.

4. Begin with the background and paint the background in shades of blue paint made by mixing colors (encourage students to experiment with the paints).

5. Complete the foreground in the same manner, using colors to reflect the ground.

6. When the watercolors have dried, draw a picture with the black marking pen onto the foreground and the background.

Extensions

1. Klee was a talented musician as well as an artist. Assign a group of students to find out about some other famous artists who also were interested in music. Tell the group to include in their report a short biography of each one, a list of their most well-known works, and the artist's connection to music. Some possible subjects include Edgar Degas, Thomas Gainsborough, and Leonardo da Vinci.

2. Through the use of color and lines, Paul Klee expressed his outlook on life. Discuss the following with the students:

    ✦ After observing a number of Klee's works, ask students to describe how they think Klee viewed life in general. What clues in his paintings led them to their conclusions?

    ✦ Henri Matisse, who also lived during the same time period as Klee, is another artist whose work evokes a dreaminess and childlike quality. Compare the work of both artists and talk about those characteristics which convey the dreamy, childlike feelings.

3. Read the following paragraph aloud to the students. Tell them to write answers to the questions below the paragraph.

    ✦ In 1937, some European artists' works were confiscated by Hitler's Nazi empire. Paul Klee was included in this spectacle. Instead of being displayed for the pleasure of the populace the works were subjected to ridicule. Derogatory comments were scrawled across the walls next to the paintings. This exhibit drew an estimated total attendace of three million people.

    ✦ Would you say this art show was a success for Nazi Germany? Why or why not? Defend your answer.

    ✦ Why do you think Hitler attempted this kind of censorship?

4. Paul Klee painted with many different paint surfaces and mediums. Each created its own special effect.

    ✦ Divide the class into five groups. Ask the groups to draw goldfish on a background using various kinds of surfaces (e.g., different kinds of cloth or a variety of textured papers). Compare the finished products. As an alternative, have each group choose a different medium with which to paint the fish scene (e.g., chalks, crayons, thick and thin tempera paints, watercolors). Have students discuss the different impressions or feelings each painting evokes. How does the medium or painting surface affect the art?

Recommended Reading _____

The Annotated Mona Lisa by Carol Strickland, Ph.D., and John Boswell (Andrews and McMeel, 1992)
Paul Klee by Ernest Raboff (Harper & Row, 1988)
Paul Klee by Mike Venezia (Children's Press, 1991)
Stories in Art by Helen Williams (Merlion Publishing, Ltd., 1991)
The Story in a Picture: Children in Art by Robin Richmond (Ideals Children's Books, 1992)

Jacob Lawrence

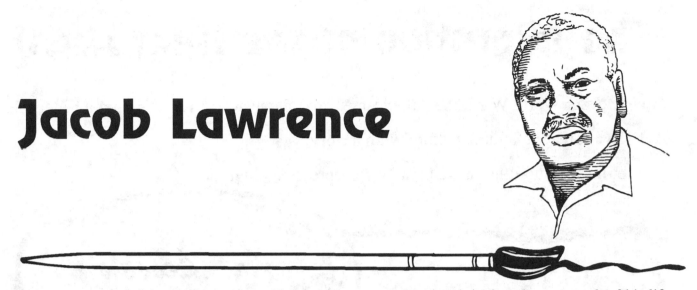

When he was only twenty-three years old Jacob Lawrence completed the best-known work of his life — *The Migration of the Negro.* Consisting of 60 individual panels this series told "...the story of an exodus of African-Americans who left their homes and farms in the South around the time of World War I and traveled to northern industrial cities in search of better lives." Today, the series is divided between two different museums. All of the even-numbered paintings can be found in The Museum of Modern Art in New York City while the odd-numbered paintings can be seen at The Phillips Collection in Washington, D.C. In 1993, a special tour to several U.S. cities reunited all 50 pieces of the Migration series.

Jacob's own life is reflective of the series' title. His parents met while they were on their separate ways north from Virginia and South Carolina. Lawrence was born in Atlantic City, New Jersey, on September 17, 1917. When he was two years old the family moved to Easton, Pennsylvania, where his father abandoned them. Later, his mother moved them to Philadelphia; they came to New York City when Jacob was 13. There, he attended an after-school arts and crafts program at the Utopia Children's House—Jacob's mother wanted him to keep busy while she was at work. Later, a full scholarship enabled him to attend the American Artists School in New York. Most of his spare time was spent in the Schomburg Collection at the New York Public Library on 135th Street where he gathered information and material to produce material for a pictorial biography of Frederick Douglass. With his subsequent Rosenwald Fellowship, Jacob was able to research southern migrants in the North after World War I. In just one year he finished his now-famous *Migration* series which is based on this research.

By his own admission Lawrence began his painting career by making designs, but gradually he began to paint street scenes reflective of the busy life around him. With the encouragement of teachers and friends, he slowly expanded his view to tell the history of the African-American in America. Through his work he intended to highlight social injustice and motivate reform. His style has been described as being a series of large, flat forms with "no depth and no details." One distinguishing feature of Jacob's paintings is his use of pure blues, reds, and yellows. In addition, each picture in the series has a title. When assembled altogether, the pictures tell a story.

Jacob Lawrence has received numerous honors and awards for his lifetime of art including the National Medal of Arts and the Spingarn Medal. In his later years he has written and illustrated two children's books—*The Great Migration* and *Harriet and the Promised Land.*

The Migration of the Negro #60

Focus: After World War I, the American Negro migrated North in search of a better life.

Activity: Creating a human mural with a story

Vocabulary: mural; narrative paintings; Depression; migration

Materials

✦ pencils

✦ paintbrushes

✦ 18" x 12" (46 cm x 30 cm) panels of white butcher paper or tagboard

✦ tempera paints (especially blue, red, and yellow)

Directions

1. Direct the students to observe Jacob Lawrence's *The Migration of the Negro* #60. Discuss the bold colors, the harshness and yet the dignity of the situation, and the lack of faces and other features on the people depicted.

2. As a class, determine a time in history that students would like to depict. Together, create a story line that will be their guide. Divide the text into manageable chunks and assign each pair or group a different piece of text to illustrate.

3. Give each pair or group a pre-cut construction paper or tagboard panel.

4. Instruct the pairs or groups to pencil sketch a picture for the text. Make sure they leave room somewhere on the page for the text itself.

5. Paint the figures on the panel. Remind the students to use lots of blue, red, and yellow.

6. Assemble the finished paintings side by side. Read the panels of the story.

Extensions

1. Read *The Great Migration* by Jacob Lawrence (published by Harper Collins, 1993). The text of this book is accompanied by pictures of all 60 of the paintings from *The Migration of the Negro* series. Also contained in this book is a poem written by Walter Dean Myers in response to Lawrence's work. After reading Myers' poem aloud to the class, direct the students to write their own response to Jacob Lawrence's migration story.

2. Discuss with the students some of the influences in Jacob Lawrence's life.

   ✦ Have them explain how Jacob's early life experiences may have contributed to his use of the migration theme in his first series.

   ✦ Find out some facts about the Depression era. What was the Great Depression, and what events caused it to happen? What was life like during that time?

3. Jacob Lawrence also wrote a children's book titled *Harriet and the Promised Land* (Simon & Schuster, 1993). This story retells in verse the mission undertaken by Harriet Tubman to lead her people to freedom in the Underground Railroad.

   ✦ Direct the students to read the book. What identifying features of Jacob Lawrence's art do they observe?

   ✦ Direct the students to write in verse and illustrate some life events of another historical African-American.

4. Paintings in *The Migration of the Negro* were done with tempera on gesso on composition board, each 18" x 12" (46 cm x 30 cm). Some were drawn horizontally and others vertically. Have the students create a painting using these same materials and measurement specifications.

5. In 1993, the exhibition *Jacob Lawrence: The Migration Series* reunited *The Migration of the Negro*. Remind the students that the 60 pictures are usually divided equally between two collections. Have them research other interesting facts about Jacob Lawrence's work. Write all the facts on a classroom chart.

6. Compare the work of Jacob Lawrence to the art of other twentieth century African-American artists, particularly Horace Pippin and Romare Bearden. Students can make Venn diagrams or a chart to show the likenesses and differences among these artists' styles.

Recommended Reading _____

The Annotated Mona Lisa by Carol Strickland, Ph.D., and John Boswell (Andrews and McMeel, 1992)

The Great Migration by Jacob Lawrence (Harper Collins, 1993)

Harriet and the Promised Land by Jacob Lawrence (Simon & Schuster, 1993)

Henri Matisse

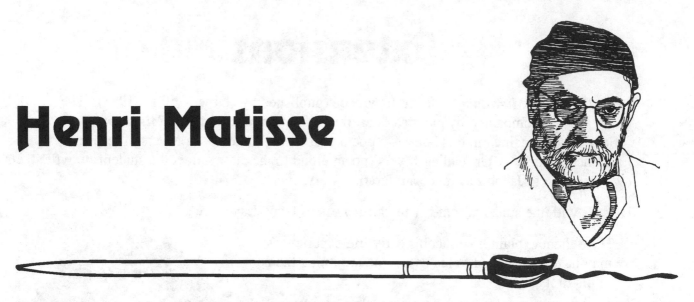

Who would have guessed that an appendectomy could lead to a career change, but that is exactly what happened to Henri Matisse. He had already trained to be a lawyer when he had to have surgery. During his recuperation period, his mother brought him some paints and a how-to book. From then on Henri was totally devoted to art. His bourgeois father was so upset and displeased with his son's decision that as Henri was leaving for Paris he yelled out, "You'll starve!"

Matisse spent a year at the Academie Julian; the next five years he studied at the Academie Carriere. During his early student years he copied the Impressionist style of painting and the Japanese style of woodblock prints. The evolution of his work continued as he discovered other groups' works. For example, while studying the Post-Impressionists, his own works became bolder and darker in time and overall were more concerned with form. Contact with Neo-Impressionists produced art work which evoked times of relaxation and pleasure. From 1913 to 1917, Matisse was briefly influenced by the Cubists with their austere, straight lines and geometrically stylized forms.

In 1904, Henri had his first one-man show, but it met with little success. By 1905, he was the leader of the Fauvist movement. Art critics at the time were alarmed by these artists' use of bright colors and distorted shapes. The critics attributed the art to work done by "wild beasts" (or Fauvists, in French). While the actual movement lasted only a few years, its effects on the art world have been felt ever since.

Throughout his long and productive career, Matisse worked twelve to fourteen hours a day, seven days a week. Besides painting, he opened his own art academy for students in 1908. That same year he published *Notes of a Painter* in which he expressed his artistic beliefs. Later, he executed murals, created stage designs for a ballet, drew several series of book illustrations, and made sculptures and collages.

Matisse was one of the first famous collage artists. His work is even more impressive when one considers that some of these works were completed while he was old, ill, and confined to bed. From his bed he instructed his assistants to paint huge pieces of paper with bright colors. Then he would cut out the shapes from the paper. As directed, his assistants pinned the shapes onto white paper and then pasted them down.

Despite the trying times in which he lived, Henri Matisse brought a special joyfulness to his art. It was his belief that an artist's painting should bring pleasure to the viewer. When Matisse died in 1954, he had more than accomplished that goal.

Beasts of the Sea

Focus: Art should bring pleasure to the viewer.

Activity: Making a collage

Vocabulary: collage; Fauvists; Cubists

Materials

- ✦ colored art tissue
- ✦ scissors
- ✦ liquid white glue
- ✦ water
- ✦ empty plastic margarine cup or other container
- ✦ paintbrushes
- ✦ tagboard or white card stock (available at copy stores)

Directions

1. With the students, discuss what forms they see in *Beasts of the Sea.* What feelings does the artist express? How do the colors, lines, and patterns contribute to this feeling?

2. In the cup, thin the glue with some water; mix.

3. Tell students to determine a theme for their collage (e.g., jungle, circus, family life, etc).

4. Have students cut out forms from the art tissue; arrange the forms on the tagboard.

5. When the arrangement is complete brush the glue over all the tissue pieces. Allow the collage to dry.

Extensions

1. As a slight variation in the lesson on page 79, have the students tear pieces of tissues rather than cut them out with the scissors. For a study in contrast, instruct the students to make two collages — one where they cut out shapes and one where they tear tissue paper shapes. Compare the two completed collages.

2. During his last years, Matisse was arthritic and confined to bed. In order to paint, charcoal was fastened to the end of a bamboo fishing stick and paper was attached to the ceiling above his bed. Henri could reach up and draw a picture. When one was finished, the paper would be taken down and another piece would be attached in its place.

   ✦ Supply each student with a piece of chalk, wooden dowel or measuring stick, and some masking tape.

   ✦ Direct the students to attach the chalk to the dowel or stick with the tape.

   ✦ Line the students in front of a chalkboard. Tell them to use their sticks to draw pictures on the board.

   ✦ Afterwards, discuss the experience with the students.

3. When Matisse's physician saw the collage, *Beasts of the Sea,* he found the colors so bright that he advised Matisse to wear dark glasses. Have the students create a bright picture using neon colored crayons or a collage using neon colored poster board or fabric. Afterwards, invite the students to bring sunglasses to school and view their works through them.

4. In 1908, Matisse published his *Notes of a Painter* in which he expressed his artistic beliefs. Have the students look at a number of Matisse's art work. With the whole group discuss what students think some of his beliefs were judging from his paintings.

5. Both Henri Matisse and Pierre Auguste Renoir painted a picture about young children who were having a piano lesson. Compare Renoir's *Young Girls at the Piano* with Matisse's *The Piano Lesson.* In which one does the subject seem to be enjoying the lesson? What can you tell from the furniture in each picture? What feelings are conveyed in each painting?

Recommended Reading _____

Henri Matisse by Ernest Raboff (Harper & Row, 1988)

Meet Matisse by Nelly Munthe (Little, Brown & Co., 1983)

The Story in a Picture: Children in Art by Robin Richmond (Ideals Children's Books, 1992)

Understanding Modern Art by Monica Bohm-Duchen and Janet Cook (EDC Publishing, 1988)

Piet Mondrian

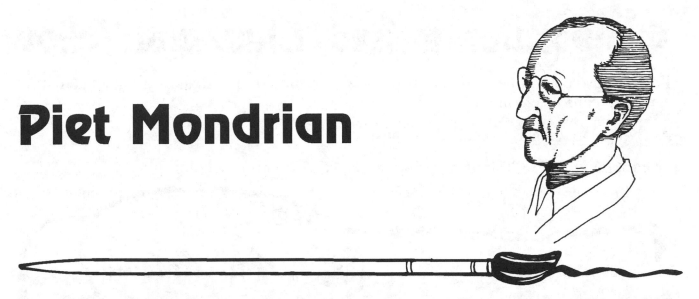

When Piet Mondrian began his art career, he painted realistic landscapes. By the time of his death in 1944, he had developed the radical, abstract style for which he is now famous. Originally he had trained to be a teacher, and he even taught for a short period of time. Then, at the age of twenty, he decided to study art. From 1892 to 1895, he attended the Amsterdam Academy. Years later, Mondrian went to Paris where he studied the Cubists and Picasso, both of whose work greatly influenced his development.

In 1914, Piet returned to Holland where he eventually founded De Stijl, or The Style, with Theo van Doesburg. De Stijl was a review of the arts based on Neo-Plasticists whose goal was to create a precise, mechanical order that seemed lacking in the natural world. It was his homeland and the effects of World War I that led Mondrian to forge this new way of thinking. Holland was a neat country with its landscape of interlocking canals and ruler-straight roads. The ensuing chaos in that country brought on by World War I led Mondrian to try to restore order to the natural world. His way of doing this was a new style of painting based on lines and rectangles.

Piet wanted art to be as mathematical as possible, a kind of blueprint for life. He filled his canvases with bold, black horizontal and vertical lines. The resulting boxes were painted with white, red, yellow, and blue. To Mondrian the vertical lines symbolized vitality while the horizontal lines represented tranquility. At first glance his grid paintings may look alike or very similar, but actually each one has been precisely calibrated and measured.

As Mondrian progressed with his unique, non-representational format, he continued to eliminate emotion from art. Colors, lines, and shapes were used for their own sake without painting an actual scene or object. So fanatical was he about his beliefs that when a fellow member of De Stijl introduced the diagonal into his paintings, Mondrian quit the society in disgust. He even transformed his own studio into one of his paintings. Walls were covered with rectangles of primary colors or white, black, and gray. All the furniture was painted white or black. He even painted his record player a bright red. One decorative figure stood out — an artificial tulip kept in a vase. Its leaves were painted white because he had banned the color green.

Today, Piet Mondrian is noted not only for his art pieces but for being one of the first to oppose subjective feeling in art. He is considered one of the most important figures in the development of abstract art.

Composition in Red, Blue, and Yellow

Focus: Use color, line, and shape for their own sakes rather than creating an actual scene or picture.

Activity: Drawing a geometric composition

Vocabulary: Neo-Plasticism; non-representational; primary colors

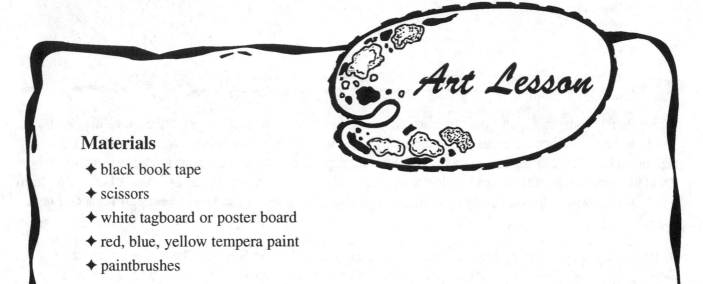

Materials

✦ black book tape

✦ scissors

✦ white tagboard or poster board

✦ red, blue, yellow tempera paint

✦ paintbrushes

Directions

1. With the students, brainstorm a list of words that describe this composition (straight, geometric, even, etc.). Notice the lines and how they are spaced. Talk about the use of color in the piece.

2. Tell the students they are going to make a Mondrian composition using black horizontal and vertical lines only and the colors red, blue, and yellow.

3. Have them cut lengths of tape and attach them to the tagboard background.

4. When students have completed the lines, have them paint some of the resulting boxes with red, blue, and yellow paint.

5. Title the completed project.

Extensions

1. As a whole group project, cover the classroom door, or one wall, or a large bulletin board with a Mondrian design. Follow these steps:

   ✦ Tape or staple white butcher paper to cover the complete surface.

   ✦ With a broad-line black marking pen and a yardstick, draw vertical and horizontal lines onto the butcher paper.

   ✦ Cut yellow, blue, and red construction paper or butcher paper to fit inside various boxes.

   ✦ Assign a group to write a brief biography of Piet Mondrian and attach it to the inside of one of the rectangles.

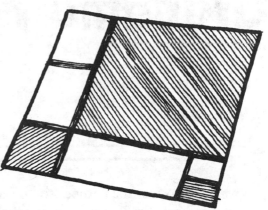

2. In his trademark paintings, Mondrian limited himself to black lines that formed rectangles and to the use of the three primary colors.

   ✦ Have the students experiment with triangular shapes instead of the rectangular shapes that characterize Mondrian's works. With a ruler and black line marker, draw numerous intersecting triangles of all sizes on a white background. Color in some of the resulting spaces with red, yellow, and blue marking pens.

   ✦ Direct the students to draw a grid of black vertical and horizontal lines on a sheet of white paper. Color in some of the spaces with the three secondary colors, green, orange, and violet. Compare this finished product with one that uses the three primary colors.

3. Challenge students to draw a design for a house that incorporates the principles outlined by Mondrian — vertical and horizontal black lines with red, yellow, and blue accents.

   Variation: Design a piece of furniture or an article of clothing that incorporates Mondrian's ideas.

4. Direct the students to cut out a small square of red, yellow, or blue paper and place it in the middle of a large sheet of white paper. Tell them to stare at the colored square for ten seconds. Have them remove the colored square while continuing to stare at that same area. They should see a square of color complementary to their original square.

Recommended Reading _____

The Annotated Mona Lisa by Carol Strickland, Ph.D., and John Boswell (Andrews and McMeel, 1992)

The Self-Portrait in Art by Sharon Lerner (Lerner Publications Company, 1965)

Understanding Modern Art by Monica Bohn-Duchen and Janet Cook (EDC Publishing, 1988)

Grandma Moses

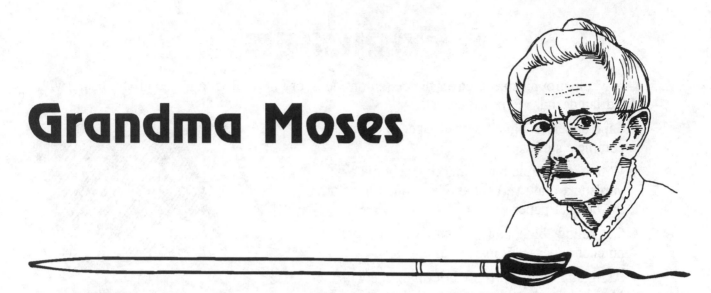

She was born Anna Mary Robertson on September 7, 1860, near Greenwich, New York, the third oldest of ten children. Little in her early years indicated the artistic path that her life would eventually follow. As a farmer's daughter she was expected to do her chores, learn how to cook and clean, and marry and raise a family of her own. Anna Mary did just that, but at an age when most folks simply retire, she took up a whole new career. Anna's paintings are still some of the most beloved pictures around, and her name is famous the world over. The story of Grandma Moses is truly inspirational.

In 1886, she worked for the James family where she met Thomas Moses; the two were married that fall. Soon after the ceremony, the newlyweds traveled by train to Virginia where they managed a farm. Anna Mary bought a cow and began to make butter. The local grocer liked this "Yankee butter" so much that he ordered it from her on a regular basis.

Homesick for his Hoosick River Valley home in New York, Thomas Moses moved his wife and five children to a farm in Eagle Bridge. Over the years, a number of new inventions invaded their simple lifestyle. Electric lights began to appear in nearby Albany in 1913, yet the Moses family chose not to install electricity until 1936. They bought their first car in 1913, but Anna preferred the horse and buggy in the country. Tragically, Thomas Moses died of a heart attack in 1927.

Grandma Moses, now 70 years old, spent some of her time stitching pictures on cloth. When one of her sisters saw how painstaking the work was, she suggested that Anna Mary paint her pictures instead. And with that one suggestion, a new career was born. One day her son, Hugh, took her work to a local drug store where women's arts and crafts could be displayed. An art collector from New York City happened to see the paintings, and he bought them all. In 1939, an art gallery owner included three of Grandma Moses' paintings in an exhibit of contemporary unknown American painters at the Metropolitan Museum of Art in New York City. They were a hit.

Grandma Moses accomplished much more in the years that followed. Hallmark Company reproduced her painting, *Out for Christmas Trees,* on one of its Christmas cards. She also wrote a book of anecdotes titled *Grandma Moses: My Life's History,* appeared on television, and gave radio interviews. Most of all, Anna Mary had shown the world that it is never too late to try something new. Anna Mary continued to paint until her death on December 13, 1961.

Sugaring Time

Focus: Grandma Moses' paintings reflected happy events in her childhood and farm life.

Activity: Drawing a snow scene

Vocabulary: primitive; landscapes; composition

Materials

- water
- tablespoons
- salt
- paint brushes
- clean plastic margarine tubs or other suitable containers
- white powdered tempera paint
- 18" x 24" (46 cm x 61 cm) drawing paper or construction paper (dark colors preferred)

Directions

1. Examine Grandma Moses' primitive style, her well-executed landscapes and flat people, and use of bright colors in her paintings. Have the students tell a story from what they see in *Sugaring Time*. Discuss sugaring off; read a description of the event from Laura Ingalls Wilder's *Little House in the Big Woods* (Harper Trophy, 1932, 1959).

2. Mix the powdered tempera and water in a margarine tub.

3. Add one tablespoon (15 mL) of salt to each tub; stir.

4. Direct the students to draw a snow scene on the paper. When the paint dries, it should appear to sparkle.

5. **Optional:** Sprinkle glitter onto the snow like Grandma Moses did on her winter scenes.

Extensions

1. When Grandma Moses was born in 1860, the United States was just entering the Civil War. Have the students research some other historic events that took place during her lifetime. Tell them to also include the date of some important inventions that happened in her lifetime, such as the electric light bulb and jet airplanes.

   ✦ As an extension, have groups of students use the researched information to make a time line that includes inventions, artists, or important events of the mid to late 1800s. Or, have student groups create collages reflective of the times. Display and discuss the groups' projects.

2. Grandma Moses' painting style is known as primitive. Establish that the word primitive here means that she was self-taught and never had an art lesson. Assign a small group of students to find other definitions of the term *primitive;* share them with the class. Have another group of students find out the names of some other famous primitive artists. List them on chart paper. Discuss what characteristic these primitive artists have in common in their works.

3. With the students, discuss how Moses used color to indicate distance and to depict seasons in her paintings.

4. Anna Mary was well known for her "Yankee butter." Students can make their own butter with this recipe. Each student will need two tablespoons (30 mL) of heavy whipping cream and an empty, clean margarine cup with a lid. Pour the cream into the cup, attach the lid, and shake vigorously. After a few minutes a solid lump of butter will form. Spread on crackers or biscuits.

5. During her 25-year art career, Grandma Moses created more than 1,500 paintings. Assign students to research ten other artists; find out if any of them were as prolific. Tell them to construct a chart or graph of their findings. Rank the artists from most works completed in a lifetime to least number of works completed in a lifetime.

6. Provide each student with a small piece of cloth (about 6"/15 cm square), a needle, and some thread. Have students draw a pencil outline of something that is especially important to them or an item that reflects a theme. Instruct students to use a basic stitch to go over the pencil outline. Have the students share their stitched art in class.

Recommended Reading _____

Barefoot in the Grass by William H. Armstrong (Doubleday & Company, Inc., 1947, 1970)

Contributions of Women: Art by Carol Fowler (Dillon Press, 1976)

Grandma Moses by Zibby O'Neal (Puffin Books, 1987)

Grandma Moses: Painter of Rural America by Donna Ruff (Viking Kestrel, 1986)

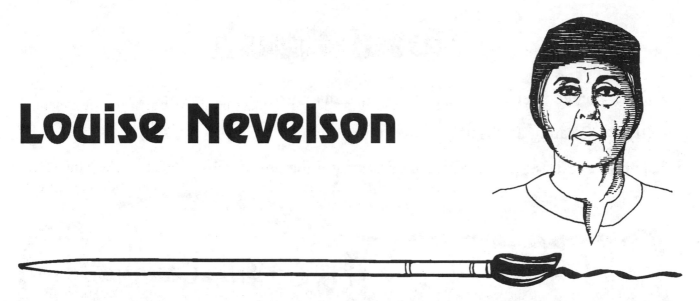

Louise Nevelson

Perhaps the first challenge in Louise's life was the move from her home in Kiev, Russia, to Rockland, Maine, in 1905, when she was only a few years old. Her father, Isaac Berliawsky, was a building contractor and lumber merchant and had emigrated two years earlier. When he sent for his family, they arrived in American wearing Persian lamb coats and were unable to speak English. Louise felt different from her schoolmates who wore wool coats and played games she did not understand. She proved to be a slow reader, and only art interested her. After school, Louise studied painting, piano, voice, and dance; she especially liked going to her father's lumberyard.

While Louise was a senior in high school, she met Charles Nevelson whom she later married. The newlyweds moved to New York City where she could study art and music. After the birth of her son, however, she found it difficult to be a wife, a mother, and an artist. Eleven years after her marriage, she chose art and separated from her husband. Louise refused any support or alimony from him. Her son, Mike, was sent to live with her parents while she went to Munich, Germany, to study Cubism with Hans Hofmann. From there she traveled through Italy and Paris to study the paintings of the masters.

After returning to New York City, she worked as an apprentice to artist Diego Rivera who painted large murals for public buildings. During this time, she began to sculpt figures and even had a job as a teacher of sculpture. When the job ended in 1941, she went to Karl Nierendorf, considered the best art dealer in New York City. She gradually sold all the jewelry she had accumulated in her marriage and was truly desperate for help. After seeing what she had created, he agreed to a showing and also offered Louise financial support so that she could continue with her work. When Nierendorf died some years later, she became severely depressed. Louise Nevelson had lost both a personal friend and her financial protector.

Nevelson recovered once again when an opportunity arose in Los Angeles for her to make lithographs of her wood sculptures. This enabled many more people to own some of her art work. Most of her assemblages (art made from odds and ends) were far too large for individuals to store. And when a particular sculpture did not sell, Louise would often dismantle the parts and use them in another piece. As Louise progressed in her career, she collected castoffs from junk shops and accumulated crates and planks to use in her assemblages. Pieces were painted one color and the insides of the compartments were filled with other wood scraps. Most of these huge monuments were not saved, but pictures of these three-dimensional art pieces attest to the format that became Louise Nevelson's unique trademark.

Royal Tide II

Focus: Found objects can be arranged within a box to create one theme.

Activity: Creating an assemblage or "art in a box"

Vocabulary: assemblage; Cubism; lithograph; theme

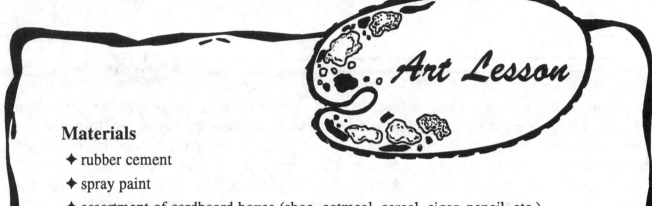

Materials

✦ rubber cement

✦ spray paint

✦ assortment of cardboard boxes (shoe, oatmeal, cereal, cigar, pencil, etc.)

✦ assortment of found objects (plastic utensils, wood scraps, dry macaroni, small toys, beads, etc.)

Directions

1. Tell the students to make a list of objects they can identify in Nevelson's *Royal Tide II* (or any of her other works). Discuss what other objects may have been appropriate to use in that particular sculpture.

2. Glue an assortment of objects inside each box. **Note:** For best results with rubber cement, apply to both the surface of the box where the object will be attached and to the area of the object which will be attached to the box. Allow the rubber cement to dry until it feels tacky; press the object to the glued surface of the box.

3. Glue the boxes together, using the same method suggested above. Spray paint the entire art piece one color.

4. Name the sculpture. Display and invite other classes to see the assemblages.

Extensions

1. Louise's father owned a lumberyard and when she was a child she played with scraps of wood she found there. With the students, discuss how this early exposure to wood may have played a role in her art career. Discuss how her career might have been different if she had grown up around a textile factory or a steel mill.

2. Louise Nevelson was the first sculptor in America to create "art in a box." One of her unusual sculptures was done on an eleven-foot (3 m) high wall. To give students an idea of the massiveness of this project, pair the students. Direct each pair to measure the height of one of the classroom walls to see if it is as tall as her sculpture.

3. As an alternative art lesson for the one presented on page 88, use this idea. Divide the students into groups of four or five. Direct each group to assemble a group sculpture that is at least their height. Assemble all of the groups' boxes together into one giant art piece. Display in the school library for all students to enjoy.

4. For a time, Louise Nevelson worked as an apprentice to Diego Rivera who was a famous painter of murals. Examine some of his work and compare it to Nevelson's. Ask students how they think Rivera's art might have influenced Nevelson's projects.

5. In Los Angeles Louise was able to make lithographs or engravings of her wood sculptures. Direct the students to write a report about lithographs and how they are made. If possible, teach the students how to make a lithograph. Invite an artist to your classroom to demonstrate the process.

6. Artist Nevelson was born in Kiev, Russia, in 1899. Direct the students to draw a map of what was then Russia; label Kiev. **Alternate activity:** Find Kiev, Russia, on a map or globe. Measure the distance from that city to students' home town.

Recommended Reading _____

Breaking Tradition: The Story of Louise Nevelson by Natalie S. Bober (Atheneum, 1984)

Contributions of Women: Art by Carol Fowler (Dillon Press Inc., 1976)

Lives of the Artists by M.B. Goffstein (Farrar, Straus Giroux, 1981)

Georgia O'Keefe

Georgia O'Keefe acknowledged that she was not much of a student, but she did enjoy her childhood on a Wisconsin farm. As the second oldest (and oldest girl) in a family of seven children, Georgia was allowed to have her own room. Her independence and unconventional ways set her apart from others. She spent many hours alone creating a fantasy world. Lessons in drawing and music furthered her imagination. When the O'Keefe sisters became skilled at drawing, their mother arranged for them to take private painting lessons. Mrs. Sarah Mann taught the girls to paint with watercolors, but when Georgia became dissatisfied with merely copying other people's work, she began to experiment on her own.

In 1902, the O'Keefe family moved from their Sun Prairie home to Williamsburg, Virginia, where they purchased a house and a general store. There Georgia would hike by herself deep into the woods to closely observe the colors and shapes in nature. Both teachers and students recognized her artistic talent; even her parents agreed that she should have more art training. A seventeen-year-old Georgia O'Keefe left for the Art Institute of Chicago in September of 1905. Four months later she ranked first in her class, despite the fact that she dreaded the embarrassing anatomy classes. Throughout her painting career, she chose to draw objects from nature rather than people.

For a few years, Georgia continued to attend art school until a series of family and personal health problems abruptly halted her formal education. Then her Aunt Ollie offered to pay for Georgia to go to Columbia Teachers' College in New York City. Life in New York was exciting and a haven for the avant-garde techniques of the Impressionists. Alfred Stieglitz, her future husband, owned a gallery called 291 where these works were displayed. It was here that Georgia's drawings were first showcased and her artistic talents first professionally recognized.

O'Keefe's paintings continued to change during the course of her life as personal events occurred and health problems arose. After her mother's death, for example, Georgie went through a blue period in which all her paintings were blue. Gradually her work became more abstract. Instead of painting a bouquet of flowers arranged in a vase, she showed the inside view of a flower. When she moved to Taos, New Mexico, her paintings reflected a desert theme.

During her lifetime, she received many awards for her work. Perhaps the most fitting was the 1979 Medal of Freedom because so much of her time had been spent fighting for personal and artistic freedom. Georgia O'Keefe died in 1986 at the age of 98.

90

Oriental Poppies

Focus: Georgia O'Keefe's flowers filled up the canvas, giving the viewer an inside look at nature.

Activity: Drawing a large picture of a flower

Vocabulary: abstract; Impressionism; avant-garde; landscape

Materials

✦ watercolors
✦ paintbrushes
✦ fresh flowers
✦ magnifying glasses
✦ pencils
✦ 12" (30 cm) square sheet of drawing paper (can be larger)

Directions

1. Observe the details of an O'Keefe flower. Notice that stems and leaves may be missing, that the inside of the flower is the part that is emphasized.

2. Direct the students to choose a fresh flower for their model and to study it in detail.

3. Have them focus on an area of flower to study with the magnifying glass.

4. When they are ready, tell the students to lightly pencil an outline of the magnified flower section on their paper. Encourage students to use up all of the paper by telling them to make sure that one section of the flower touches each of the edges of the paper.

5. Paint the flowers using watercolors. Allow the flowers to dry.

6. Display each painting with its real flower.

Extensions

1. In one of her paintings, Georgia placed a pink rose in the eye socket of of a horse's skull. Art critics loved the way she mixed art and death in these skull paintings. Challenge students to mix art and death in a composition. Pair or group the students and have them create a display of something dead with something live (e.g., chicken bones and leaves). Tell them to name their work. Groups can walk around to view one another's projects.

2. During her lifetime, Georgia painted over 900 works of art. Direct the students to research and find the names of other artists who were as prolific as she was.

3. After her mother's death, Georgia went through a blue period in which everything she painted was blue.

   ✦ Discuss with students why this was an especially appropriate color for her to use.

   ✦ Ask students which colors they might use if they were happy, sad, angry, frightened, or any other feeling.

   ✦ Research and name some other artists who went through a blue period.

4. Georgia liked to paint natural objects. Pair the students and take them on a nature walk around the school neighborhood. When you return to the classroom, assign the following activities.

   ✦ Have them write a list of all the things they see that would make an interesting topic for a nature painting.

   ✦ Follow up by letting them draw or paint pictures of one thing that interested them most. Have students assemble the pictures into a folder or book.

5. Both Mary Cassatt and Georgia O'Keefe faced prejudice from the art community. Tell how each one dealt with these prejudices. Discuss any prejudices facing female artists today.

Recommended Reading _____

Georgia O'Keefe by Jacqueline A. Ball (Blackbird Press, 1991)

Georgia O'Keefe, Painter by Michael Berry (Chelsea House, 1988)

Georgia O'Keefe by Robyn Turner (Little, Brown and Company, 1991)

Inspirations: Stories About Women Artists by Leslie Sills (Albert Whitman and Company, 1989)

Masterpieces of American Art: A Fact-Filled Coloring Book by Alan Gartenhaus (Running Press, 1992)

Pablo Picasso

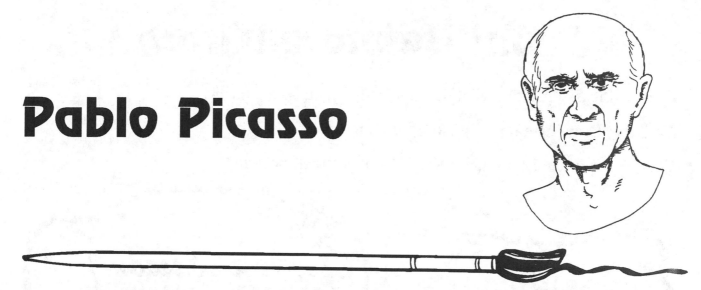

As a painter and a sculptor, it is not untrue to say that Pablo Picasso revolutionized 20th century art. With his close collaborator, Braque, he developed a completely new type of painting known as Cubism.

Picasso was born on October 25, 1881, in Malaga, Spain; he was the oldest of three children and the only male. His father, Don Jose, was an art teacher who possessed modest talent. He did, however, have a flair for the unusual and colorful. He once stuck cut-out birds to the surface of a painting. Undoubtedly this influenced Pablo's ideas later in life. When Don Jose realized the extent of his son's talent he turned over his brushes to the boy and vowed never to paint again!

When the family moved to Barcelona in 1895, Pablo passed the entrance requirements at the art school in just one day, a procedure normally taking about one month. Two years later at the Royal Academy in Madrid, Picasso repeated his amazing performance. With nothing left to be learned at these establishments, he began to study the masterpieces on his own and eventually decided to go to England. On the way there he stopped in Paris, France, the greatest center of European art at that time. Here he could study first-hand the art of Van Gogh, Munch, and Toulouse-Lautrec as well as meet other artists and writers. It was a time of hardship and poverty for him which was reflected in his work during this period. Since everything was painted in ghostly blues, the term "Blue Period" is used to describe his body of painting from 1901 to 1904.

After his blue period, Picasso developed a brand new kind of painting known as Cubism. Until this way of painting surfaced, objects were depicted as if seen from the viewfinder of a camera. With the advent of photography, however, artists were able to explore beyond external appearances. Painters began to flatten out and reassemble images on the canvas; paintings no longer had only one point of view. Cubism brought the greatest change that the art world had seen in over five centuries.

The outbreak of World War I in 1914 brought many changes to Picasso's life. Many of his peers were drafted; a favorite friend and great champion of Cubism never recovered from a head wound. A second world war brought about the epic painting, *Guernica,* which displayed Picasso's feelings about the horrors of war.

Throughout the latter part of his life, Picasso enjoyed fame and wealth and continued to create art until his death on April 9, 1973. His works have received worldwide acclaim, and his influence can still be felt in the art community today.

Girl Before a Mirror

Focus: Picasso painted what he knew rather than what he saw.

Activity: Drawing a portrait using the elements of Cubism

Vocabulary: Cubist; collage; Surrealism; abstract; portrait

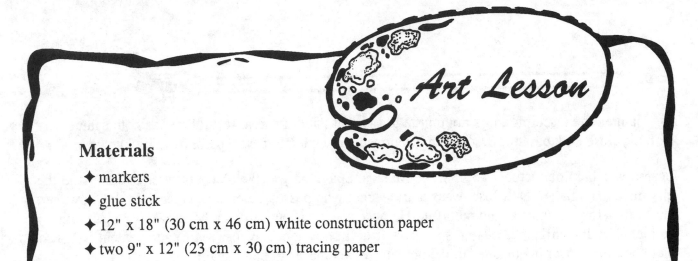

Art Lesson

Materials

✦ markers
✦ glue stick
✦ 12" x 18" (30 cm x 46 cm) white construction paper
✦ two 9" x 12" (23 cm x 30 cm) tracing paper

Directions

1. Have students fold each sheet of tracing paper into fourths. Open the sheets.

2. Ask students to draw a profile on one of these sheets of tracing paper. Use this profile to help you draw your profile by sections. Notice where the features are placed according to other shapes around them.

3. Instruct students to draw a front view of a portrait on the other sheet of tracing paper. Use this pattern to help you draw the portrait by sections.

4. Trace one of the drawings onto the other.

5. Color in each enclosed area. Outline all the pencil lines with a thick black marker.

6. Use a glue stick to mount the completed pattern onto the 12" x 18" (30 cm x 46 cm) construction paper for a mat.

Extensions

1. As a variation of the art lesson on page 94, have the students draw a self-portrait. Provide a mirror large enough for them to view their whole faces. Drawing can proceed in the same manner as outlined on that page.

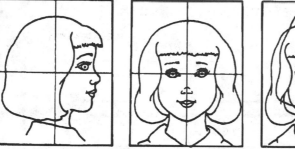  

2. Picasso went through a "Blue Period" from 1901 to 1904 in which his art was done in tones of blue. Have the students give reasons why they think his art work at this time was all one color. Discuss possible reasons why Picasso might have chosen blue rather than green or red or another color.

3. In the early 1900s, Picasso befriended Leo Stein, an American art collector, and his sister Gertrude, a well-known writer. Assign the students to find out more about Picasso's relationship with the Steins. Have them name some of Gertrude's more famous works.

4. Some contemporaries of Pablo Picasso include Albert Einstein, Sigmund Freud, Alexander Graham Bell, Hitler, Jackson Pollock, Henri Matisse, and Henry Ford. Divide the class into small groups and direct them to create a time line of famous people who lived and events that took place during Picasso's lifetime (1881–1973).

5. In 1912, Picasso concentrated on collages, pictures made by attaching fabric, paper, and other materials to a background. Direct the students to make a food collage. Start with crackers and garnish with pickle slices, radish rounds, cream cheese and cucumber slices (or other foods). Let students share their edible collage with a partner before eating it!

6. Write the following words on the chalkboard or overhead projector for all to view: abstract, surrealism, collage, cubism, fauvism. Instruct the students to define each one. Encourage the use of art books and magazines to find definitions.

Recommended Reading _____

Famous People by Kenneth and Valerie McLeish (Troll Associates, 1991)

First Impressions: Pablo Picasso by John Beardsley (Harry N. Abrams, 1991)

Pablo Picasso by Patricia A. MacDonald (Silver Burdett Press, 1990)

Pablo Picasso by Ernest Raboff (Doubleday, 1982)

Picasso by Mike Venezia (Children's Press, 1988)

Picasso and His World by Terry Measham (Silver Burdett Press, 1980)

Horace Pippin

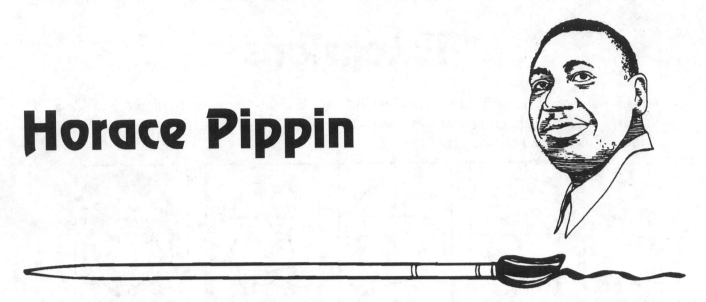

Horace Pippin was born on February 22, 1888, in West Chester, Pennsylvania. As a child, he attended a one-room "colored" school which housed first through eighth grades. It was there that Horace began drawing sketches of his spelling words — an act which earned him detention. That did not deter his drawing activities, however. One day he noticed an ad in a magazine that offered a prize for drawing a funny face. Horace entered the contest and the following week was awarded a box of six colored crayons, a box of cold waterpaint and two brushes.

When Horace was fourteen, his mother remarried. Horace was sent to work on the farm of Mr. James Gavin who recognized Horace's talent and offered to send him to art school. Horace was unable to accept the offer because his mother became ill; he returned to town to be closer to his ailing mother. During this time, he accepted odd jobs of any kind. When World War I broke out, Horace joined the Army where he was assigned to the 369th Infantry Regiment. This unit was comprised solely of black soldiers whose assignment in France was to build 500 miles of railroad track inland from the sea. When the French and British armies were in danger of being crushed and not enough American soldiers had arrived, the French quickly trained the 369th for combat duty. In the course of battle, Horace's right arm was pierced and paralyzed by a sniper's bullet.

After returning to the United States, Pippin could no longer perform the work of the job he had left behind, so he decided to visit his brother John. There he met Ora Jennie Featherstone Wade, a twice-widowed woman with a young son. The two married and survived on Horace's meager disability pension and Ora Jennie's laundry work. In constant pain, Horace could no longer paint until he found a way to control his brush stroke. Holding the injured right wrist in the fist of his left hand, he was able to use tiny brush strokes. For three years he worked on his first canvas and called it *End of the War: Starting Home.*

In 1937, the West Chester County Art Association held its annual art show, and Horace Pippin entered two paintings. This marked the first time a black artist's paintings had ever been accepted at the show. It also brought Horace instant success. With success came a series of changes in his life. His wife had to be committed to a mental institution. Horace took to drinking and staying out late. After one such late evening, he died in his sleep; the official cause of death was listed as a "stopped heart." On July 6, 1946, the world lost a talent who overcame a crippling injury to do what he knew best.

End of the War: Starting Home

Focus: Horace Pippin drew pictures of his life experiences as a poor black child and as a wounded hero in a segregated army.

Activity: Draw a picture of an important life experience

Vocabulary: primitive; segregated; one-man show

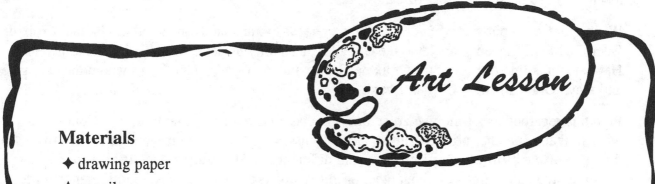

Materials

✦ drawing paper

✦ pencils

✦ colored marking pens or pencils

Directions

1. Encourage students to discuss some important events in their lives — events that have left an impression on them and that will last a long time. Tell them to choose one event as the topic of their drawing.

2. Direct the students to sketch an outline of the picture using a pencil.

3. When students are satisfied with their drawings, have them fill in the shapes with colored pens or pencils.

4. Have each student give his/her completed picture an appropriate title.

5. For those students who wish to share the events that prompted the sketches, have them write about the events on an index card. Display the cards along with the titled drawings. (Allow time for students to share the pictures within small groups, or as a class, before displaying all of them on a bulletin board or wall.)

Extensions

1. William H. Johnson is another African-American artist who paints in the same style as Horace Pippin. Read about Johnson in *Li'l Sis and Uncle Willie* by Gwen Everett (National Museum of American Art, 1991). Compare the drawings and subject matter of both artists.

2. When Pippin joined the Army during World War I, blacks and whites were segregated. Discuss how the situation has changed today, if prejudices still exist in the armed services, and what advances have been made for African-Americans.

3. When Horace Pippin was wounded in the war, he was immediately awarded the French Croix de Guerre. Twenty-seven years later, the United States Army presented him with the Purple Heart. Have students find out about the Croix de Guerre and the Purple Heart — to whom they are given and why. Draw a picture of each award.

4. Pippin is regarded as a primitive artist, one who has received no formal training. Compare his work to that of another primitive artist, Henri Rousseau. How are their works alike? How do they differ? Make a chart of these likenesses and differences. **Alternative Activity:** Assign each group of students to find out about other primitive artists such as Frida Kahlo or Grandma Moses. As a whole group, determine common characteristics of all the primitive artists who were researched.

5. Examine some other art pieces that depict World War I. Compare them with those drawn by Horace Pippin. Ask students to describe or characterize the war as seen through the eyes of the various artists.

6. "It is the year 1919 and you have just been discharged from the Army. Your right arm, your drawing arm, has been paralyzed by a sniper's bullet. You can no longer do the work you were doing when you left for the war. The pain is constant, and you would give anything to be able to draw again." After presenting this scenario to students, have them write a story or diary entries describing their struggle to continue their artistic endeavors.

7. Direct the students to find out about some other great African-American artists in America. In their reports, have them include any adversities that had to be overcome, including schooling, prejudices, lack of money, or personal problems. Along with each report students should include a drawing they have made using the same style as the artist.

Recommended Reading _____

Great Negroes, Past and Present by Russell L. Adams (Afro-Am, Inc., 3rd revised edition, 1984)

Horace Pippin: The Artist as a Black American by Selden Rodman and Carole Cleaver (Doubleday & Company, Inc., 1972)

Tammy Rahr

Traditional artist Tammy Rahr is a member of the Cayuga Nation that originally occupied what is now New York State. The Cayuga is one of the six nations that composed the Iroquois Confederacy. A progressive people, the Iroquois established one of the first democracies in the world and allowed women an equal say, or the vote, centuries before European countries ever considered the idea. Their leaders were renowned for their diplomacy. In fact, the founding fathers of America borrowed many of the Iroquois' ideas about governing and incorporated them into the Constitution. It comes as no surprise, then, that Tammy Rahr has established herself as a highly respected artist and spokeswoman for native rights.

During her childhood years Tammy spent a lot of time outdoors making things from leaves, flowers, and dirt. Then the family moved from the woodlands of New York State to an urban city outside of Los Angeles, California. The experience made her more aware of what was going on in the world. After returning to New York with her family, Tammy faced another lesson in growing up. A gifted student, she was sent to college when she was just 14. Tammy was able to earn her high school diploma and some college credit before quitting and trying her hand at a number of different jobs. Eventually, she and her son, David John, moved to Santa Fe, New Mexico, so that she could study at the Institute of American Indian Arts. After graduating from the institute she remained active with it and the museum there.

Through her bead work, corn husk dolls, and cradleboards, Tammy Rahr's goal is to create toys that combine traditional Native American with modern American toys. She feels that this is one important way to show Native American children that their traditional ways are equal to the new ones. For example, she puts modern dolls on her cradleboards. Another theme in her art is the preservation of the natural world. Tammy feels that many of Earth's plants and trees are being threatened and we must care for them. Images of various flowers and trees can be found on the cradleboards that she creates.

Tammy's art has won first place awards at the famous Santa Fe Indian Market. She has also presented her works in a show at the Smithsonian Institution in New York. Now in her thirties, Tammy Rahr continues to create art that is both pleasing to look at and meaningful.

A Cradleboard

Focus: Preservation of the natural world is an important aspect of Rahr's art.

Activity: Making a type of cradleboard

Vocabulary: Iroquois Confederacy; Cayuga; traditional arts

Materials

- ✦ round paper plates
- ✦ scissors
- ✦ stapler
- ✦ colored pencils or marking pens
- ✦ twigs, flowers, feathers, and other natural objects

Directions

1. Have the students look at the images on Tammy Rahr's cradleboard. Can they identify the flowers or any of the materials used to construct the cradleboard?

2. Give each pair of students three paper plates. Tell them to cut one plate in half so that each partner has one whole plate and one-half of a plate.

3. Place the half plate on a flat working surface so that its rounded side faces up.

4. Direct the students to decorate this half with pictures of things in nature. Use Tammy Rahr's cradleboard as an example of what to draw.

5. When the half plate is decorated, position it over the bottom half of the whole plate to form a pocket.

6. Staple the half plate to the whole plate around the edges where the two plates meet.

7. Fill the pocket with twigs, feathers, flowers, or other natural objects.

8. If desired, punch two holes near the top of the whole plate and thread a length of yarn through them. Tie the ends of the yarn in a bow and hang the cradleboard for display.

Extensions

1. Learn how to make some other traditional art such as beadwork or yarn painting. Complete directions can be found in *Native Artists of North America* by Reavis Moore (John Muir Publication, 1993).

2. Invite any local traditional artists to share their work with your class. If none are available, have your librarian help you locate books that depict Native American art. Or, find out if there is a display of native art in your area that your class could visit.

3. The Iroquois Confederacy was composed of six nations.

    ✦ Assign some students to find out the names of all six nations.

    ✦ The Iroquois were noted for their goodwill. Have the students do research to find out how the Tuscarora nation became part of the confederacy.

    ✦ Iroquois is actually a French word. Assign some students to find out about some of the early French explorers and missionaries who came in contact with the Iroquois (e.g., Jacques Cartier and Champlain).

4. People of the Iroquois Confederacy call themselves Haudenosaunee or "the people of the Long Houses." Find pictures of long houses to show to the students. Challenge them to draw a diagram or build a model of a long house. Students can be grouped for this activity.

5. Read aloud "Law of the Great Peace" (adapted by John Bierhorst; from *The Big Book of Peace*, edited by Ann Durell and Marilyn Sachs, published by Dutton Childrens Books, 1990). The students can complete any of the following activities.

    ✦ Explain why you think the tree was chosen as a symbol of peace. Draw a picture of other plants or animals that you think symbolize peace.

    ✦ Find the statement that is similar to Abraham Lincoln's line that we are all created equal.

    ✦ In groups, write laws of peace for the classroom. Title them "Peace Begins with You," and place the set of laws in book. Share your peace books with the class.

Recommended Reading

"Law of the Great Peace" adapted by John Bierhorst, ed. by Ann Durell and Marily Sachs. *The Big Book of Peace* (Dutton Childrens Books, 1990)

Native Artists of North America by Reavis Moore (John Muir Publications, 1993)

Faith Ringgold

Artist Faith Ringgold was born into the Depression in the year 1930. Her father, Andrew Jones, was a sanitation engineer in New York City while her mother, Willi Posey Jones, was a fashion designer and dressmaker. Besides Faith there were two older children in the family. As a child, Faith was sickly and suffered from asthma which often kept her from attending school. To help her recover, Faith's mother brought her crayons and paper, needles and thread, and fabric and encouraged her to express herself creatively. Mrs. Jones also took Faith on downtown outings to museums and to see stars such as Benny Goodman, Duke Ellington, and Judy Garland. It was during these excursions that Faith determined that she, too, would be a star some day.

Following the footsteps of her grandparents, Ms. Ringgold entered the school of education to become a teacher. Her goal was to teach art and have spare time to create her own art work.

For some twenty years, Faith taught grades kindergarten through college. During this time, she became interested in the political writings of some black authors, including those of her brother, James Baldwin. These writings inspired her to paint a mosaic of one hundred faces — 98 white and two black — to show that inequality is wrong. Faith called these paintings the "American People Series." Through demonstrations, she and others convinced museums to exhibit the work of some black female artists.

In 1972, a question from one of her students altered the course of her career. The student did not understand why Faith used watercolors in her paintings instead of the beads and fabrics she encouraged her classes to utilize. Faith realized that she had been ignoring her African culture and heritage. That summer she traveled to Europe where she visited an art museum that featured Tibetan paintings mounted on cloth. After arriving home, she quit her teaching career and began to work full time on her art. Her first project was a series of masks which could be hung from a ceiling or a wall. Gradually she began to make soft art sculpture and later on, quilts. These quilts were part autobiographical, part painting, and part story which told of her experience as a black female in America.

Faith gained national attention in the early 1980s when she had a major exhibition of her work from the past twenty years. The University of California in San Diego invited her to be a full professor there. She retains that position half the year and lives in the Sugar Hill section in New York City the remainder of the year. In addition to these accomplishments, Faith Ringgold has written and illustrated two children's books: *Aunt Harriet's Underground Railroad in the Sky* and *Tar Beach*. The latter was her first picture book and won a Caldecott Medal in 1991.

Tar Beach

Focus: Through her quilts, Faith Ringgold expressed her feelings and experiences as a black female in America.

Activity: Creating a quilt

Vocabulary: soft sculpture; tampas; quilts

Art Lesson

Materials

✦ assortment of fabric pieces

✦ scissors

✦ white art tissue paper

✦ pencils

✦ black, thick-line marking pens

✦ colored marking pens, or needles and colored threads

Directions

1. Give students ample opportunity to examine one of Faith Ringgold's quilts from *Tar Beach* (Crown Publishers, Inc., 1992). Discuss the actions taking place in the various sections of the quilt.

2. Direct the students to think of some event in their lives that has been especially important or meaningful to them. Have them use pencil to sketch a drawing of the event onto the white art tissue.

3. Cut a fabric square to the same size as the drawing.

4. Place the tissue over the fabric, and with the blackline marker trace over the pencil lines. The marker will bleed through to the fabric.

5. With the colored marking pens or the needle and thread, trace the lines made by the black marking pen. Fill the interior spaces with color pens or glue fabric scraps to them.

6. Sew all the students' fabric pieces into one large quilt.

Extensions

1. Assign students to read Faith Ringgold's picture books: *Tar Beach* (Crown Publishers, Inc., 1991) and *Aunt Harriet's Underground Railroad in the Sky* (Crown Publishers, Inc., 1992). Compare and contrast the illustrations of both books. Discuss how Ms. Ringgold's heritage has influenced her art.

2. Make soft sculptures. Each student will need a piece of fabric, scissors, needle and thread, and newspaper or tissue for stuffing material.
   - ✦ Fold the fabric piece in half.
   - ✦ Cut out a shape (a star, a fish, etc.) through both layers of the fabric, leaving the fold intact.
   - ✦ Turn the fabric inside out and sew all the edges together, leaving a small opening for stuffing.
   - ✦ Turn the fabric right-side out and stuff with crumpled newspaper or tissue.
   - ✦ Sew up the hole. Attach a thread to each sculpture and hang them from the classroom ceiling.

3. Research the history of quilt-making in Colonial America. Find out what patterns were used, how the quilts were constructed, the importance of a quilting bee, etc. Look at some books which contain pictures of these quilts; discuss what stories they tell.

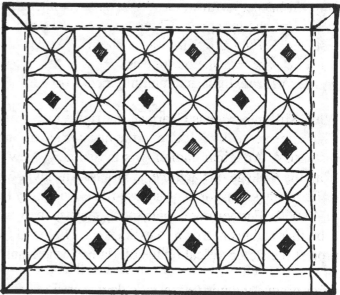

4. Set the mood while the students are making their quilts (see art lesson on page 103) by playing background music. Choose from Benny Goodman, Duke Ellington, or Judy Garland — the same musicians who inspired Faith Ringgold as a child.

5. The quilts featured in *Tar Beach* are taken from Ms. Ringgold's "Woman on a Bridge" series. If possible, display a book that contains all five quilts in that series.

6. Faith's grandparents were teachers, and her mother was a fashion designer and dressmaker. With the students, discuss how Faith's relatives' occupations may have influenced her career.

Recommended Reading _____

Aunt Harriet's Underground Railroad in the Sky by Faith Ringgold (Crown Publishers, Inc., 1992)

Inspirations: Stories About Women Artists by Leslie Sills (Albert Whitman, 1989)

Tar Beach by Faith Ringgold (Crown Publishers, Inc., 1991)

Charlene Teters

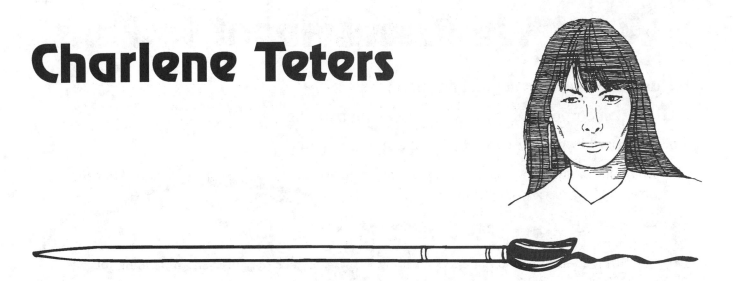

Native American artist Charlene Teters was born and raised in Spokane, Washington. Her mother was from the Spokane tribe and her father was Dutch. Throughout her childhood, Charlene spent much of her time visiting relatives on the reservation, particularly her grandmother's house. This house was typical of homes on the reservation. There was no indoor plumbing so on weekends Charlene would help fill buckets with water for her grandmother to have on hand. The inside walls were covered with cardboard and tar paper. Charlene remembers that when she was 12 years old, electricity was finally installed. When Charlene was in the fifth grade, she began to realize that not everyone's grandmother was like hers, and she became ashamed of her. Years later Charlene came to realize what a treasure her grandmother really was. Within her own tribe, Grandmother was an honored storyteller.

While still in her teens Charlene married a man from a nearby tribe. They had two children, but Charlene eventually left due to the abusive situation. Soon after, she began her art studies at the Institute of American Indian Arts in Santa Fe, New Mexico. After completing a bachelor of arts degree from the College of Santa Fe, Charlene was invited to study at the University of Illinois. It was a difficult transition for her because there were only three Native Americans in a student body population of 40,000. Furthermore, their sports team name was the Fighting Illini, named after a Native American tribe that had been driven to extinction. Offended by the team mascot, Charlene was not afraid to protest the stereotypical image of Native Americans portrayed at the University.

After graduating with a master's degree in fine arts, Ms. Teters returned to the Institute of American Indian Arts where her role consists of working closely with artists from other Native American tribes. Primarily a painter, Charlene likes to incorporate objects with her art. Her self-proclaimed purpose is to address issues of human dignity and freedom and to cause people to think. In addition to her art, Charlene Teters has become an educator and a spokeswoman for Native Americans.

What We Know About Indians

Focus: Indian people are real people.

Activity: Incorporating cartoon images with paintings

Vocabulary: Spokane tribe; culture; communication

Art Lesson

Materials

✦ scissors

✦ glue

✦ colored marking pens

✦ clear plastic wrap or clear acetate sheets

✦ clear tape

✦ sheet of white construction paper or tagboard

✦ old magazines or photographs (preferably portraits)

Directions

1. Charlene Teters' art work often reflects how false images hide the true identity of native people. Draw the students' attention to this fact as they observe *What We Know About Indians*. Discuss with the class what that picture says about Native Americans.

2. Direct the students to find an old photograph or a portrait to cut out and glue to the construction paper or tagboard.

3. Cut a piece of plastic wrap or acetate to the size of the construction paper or tagboard.

4. Tape the plastic wrap or acetate to the construction paper or tagboard along the top of the page.

5. Tell the students to use marking pens to draw cartoon images directly onto the plastic wrap or acetate. These images should reflect stereotypes of the person in the portrait.

6. Add appropriate words, numbers, or phrases if desired.

7. Title the work "What We Know About... "

8. View the pictures by carefully lifting the plastic sheets or acetate that cover the portraits; return the covering to its original position after viewing.

Extensions

1. Brainstorm a list of stereotypes that people may have about different cultures. With the class discuss why this kind of generalizing is unfair, harmful, and full of misconceptions and untruths. Ask them why they think people sometimes stereotype others and what can be done to correct this type of thinking.

2. Assign a group of students to research the Spokane way of life. Direct them to draw pictures of the native dress; make a list of the beliefs; describe the customs. Have them present their findings in an oral report to the rest of the class.

3. Charlene Teter's grandmother was a respected storyteller in her tribe. Read some Native American stories such as *Buffalo Woman* by Paul Goble (Bradbury Press, 1984); *Knots on a Counting Rope* by Bill Martin Jr. and John Archambault (Henry Holt and Company, 1987); *The Legend of the Bluebonnet* by Tomie dePaola (G.P. Putnam's Sons, 1983). Afterwards, group the students and let them write their own Native American stories.

4. Write this quote by Charlene Teters on the chalkboard for all to see:

   ✦ "I believe that art is the highest form of communication. Artists have always been the conscience of their nations."

   ✦ Have the students write a response to her statement. Let them share their responses with a partner.

5. Find Spokane, Washington, on a map. Direct the students to find other evidences of Native American names in the state of Washington (names of cities, rivers, etc.). Tell them to find out about any other Native American tribes in the Washington area, especially those headed by Chief Seattle. Direct them to write a paragraph outlining Chief Seattle's lifetime achievements.

6. When Charlene attended the University of Illinois the sports team was the Fighting Illini.

   ✦ Assign a group of students to find out who the Illini were and how they were driven to extinction.

   ✦ Charlene objected to the use of a Native American stereotype to represent the school's sports team. Write a letter to the University of Illinois protesting the continued use of this image.

Recommended Reading _____

Brother Eagle, Sister Sky, a Message from Chief Seattle (Dial Books, 1991)
Native Artists of North America by Reavis Moore (John Muir Publications, 1993)

Wang Yani

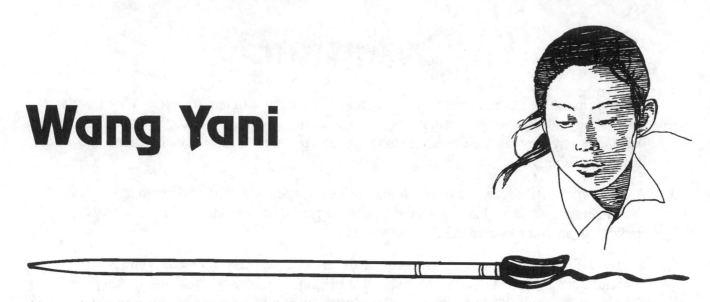

At age sixteen this talented young woman was already being called the Picasso of China. She held her first major exhibition in Shanghai at the age of four and since then has solo exhibited in Great Britain, the United States, Japan, and Germany. In addition, she excels in a number of styles, including impressionism, scribble, geometric, and rustic. During her short lifetime, she has produced over 10,000 paintings. Wang Yani is truly a remarkable artist.

Yani was born in Gongcheng, China, in 1975, and is the older of two children. Her mother, Tang Fenjiao, worked in the toy department of a store; her father, Wang Shiqiang, was an art educator and an artist in his own right. Much of Yani's success can be attributed to her father who is alternately strict and encouraging of Yani's talent. This artist's story began when a two-year-old Yani accompanied her father to his art studio. There she picked up a piece of charcoal and began to make scribbles on the wall. Rather than scold Yani, her father offered her a pencil and paper. He was amazed with her drawings and the quick progress she made in her artistic development.

When Yani entered primary school at age seven, she showed signs of shyness. To encourage her to overcome her timidness and to help her become bold with her art work, her father provided her with large brushes and huge sheets of paper, some of them larger than Yani!

To stimulate Yani's mental growth and imagination, Yani's father took her to many interesting places, including the Great Wall of China, Palace Museum in Beijing, and Confucian Temple in Qufu, Shangdong Province. With her childhood drawing to a close, her paintings also grew broader in subject matter. At first, her paintings had captured the feelings of love between parents and children. As she was given opportunities to play with other children, her work began to include birds and other animals which represented children at play. Now in her teens, Yani has shown greater interest in flowers, mountains, people, birds, fish, and other creatures.

Today Yani continues to paint, often while listening to music on her Walkman. Her favorite music includes Chinese, Schubert, Mozart, and Beethoven's Fifth Symphony. Yani still paints from memory and her feelings and impressions come through clearly. In her spare time, she reads Chinese literature, plays musical instruments, writes poetry, sings and dances, and studies the English language. Truly, she is one of China's greatest treasures.

Lion Is Awake!

Focus: Animals are used by Wang Yani to represent children at play.

Activity: Drawing animals at play

Vocabulary: ca; jimo; pomo; cun; poumo

Materials

✦ pencils

✦ brushes of various sizes

✦ watercolors

✦ 12" x 18" (30 cm x 46 cm) or larger sheet of butcher paper

Directions

1. Display a copy of *Lion Is Awake!* (available in the February, 1990, issue of *Instructor*). Ask students to tell about the action in the picture. What events do they think happened before the artist captured this scene? What do they think might happen next? Have them speculate on what is written in the inscription at the bottom of the picture. Read aloud the translation of the actual inscription.

2. Tell the students to crumple the paper. Smooth it out before beginning to draw on it.

3. Direct the students to lightly draw in pencil some children at play; tell them to use their favorite animals to represent the children.

4. Paint the figures with the watercolors.

5. After they have completed the project, they may write an inscription, just like Yani did, at the bottom of the picture.

6. In whole group share the watercolors and their accompanying stories.

7. You may want to play background music while the students work. Choose from Chinese music or the works of Schubert, Mozart, or Beethoven (Yani's own favorites).

Extensions

1. Wang Yani was a child prodigy. With the students, talk about the meaning of prodigy. Who are some other famous child prodigies?

2. Establish that traditional Chinese painting captures the idea or spirit of what an artist sees — somewhat similar to Impressionist art. Chinese painting is not so much concerned with perspective as it is with the arrangement of black or colored areas with blank spaces. Examine some other Chinese drawings and paintings by various painters; find these elements in the drawings and paintings.

3. Many Chinese paintings contain inscriptions; an *inscription* is a poem or short story about the ideas presented in a painting. Divide the class into pairs or small groups. Provide each one with a different print to observe. Tell students to write a poem or story about their picture. This activity can also be done on an individual basis; assign the students to find their own pictures to write about.

4. Have the students find out about these texture strokes used by traditional Chinese artists: cun, ca, and dotting. Tell the students to define each term and to provide a sample of each. For information on these terms, see the book in the listing below, *How to Draw with Pen & Brush*.

5. Ink can be used in a variety of ways to produce different effects. Have the students explore the jimo, pomo, and poumo techniques. Tell them to find out what each one is; see if they can identify each in one of Wang Yani's pictures. These terms are explained in *A Young Painter* by Zheng Zhensun and Alice Low (Scholastic Inc., 1991).

6. For a variation on the art lesson on page 109, try either of the following techniques utilized by Chinese artists.
   ✦ Spray the drawing paper with water before painting on the surface.
   ✦ Put something with a textured surface underneath the drawing paper.

7. Have students practice brush strokes as they experience the artistic grace and form of Chinese writing. Make a large Chinese Zodiac calendar. Label each section with the name of an animal (see diagram at right). Divide the class into small groups and assign each group a calendar animal. Have groups recreate the Chinese characters on the classroom Zodiac calendar. **Optional:** Ask each group to paint a picture of the animal and display it on or near the calendar.

Recommended Reading _____

How to Draw with Pen & Brush by Arthur Zaidenberg (Vanguard Press, 1965)

Instructor Magazine, February 1990 issue (contains a poster of *Lion is Awake!*)

People in Art by Anthea Peppin (The Millbrook Press, 1991)

A Young Painter by Zheng Zhensun and Alice Low (Scholastic Inc., 1991)

Culminating Activities

Complete your studies about artists with one of the following culminating activity suggestions:

1. Direct the students to choose a favorite artist and create an art project that reflects that artist's style. Also have them write two or more paragraphs explaining why they like that artist's style and what characteristics of the artist they most admired. Make a wall display of all projects and paragraphs.

2. Create an artists' quilt. Assign each student a different artist. Have them cut out fabric shapes to represent that artist's style (for example, cubes for Picasso) and attach them to a burlap square. Sew or embroider the artist's name on the square. Tape or sew all the squares together; display the quilt on a wall.

   On a long sheet of butcher paper, make a list of all the different art movements through the ages, beginning with the Renaissance. (Leave enough room between listings to write in the names of various artists who lived at that time.) Beside each artist's name write the date of birth and death and the names of some of their most famous art works.

3. Create an "Art Through the Ages" display. Divide the class into groups. Assign each group a particular style of art inspired by a movement (e.g., Impressionism, Cubism, Surrealism, Expressionism). Try to include art from the Renaissance and Baroque periods as well as the nineteenth and twentieth centuries. Each group should make a sketch representative of the style to which it has been assigned. (Provide copies of art and necessary supplies for the groups.) When all groups have completed their projects, display the art, along with the artists (groups) names and titles of the pieces, on a large wall in the classroom (or a school library, lobby, multipurpose room, etc.)

Bibliography

Behr, Shulamith. *Women Expressionists*. Rizzoli, 1988

Blizzard, Gladys S. *Come Look with Me*. Thomasson-Grant, 1990

Bohm-Duchen, Monica and Janet Cook. *An Usborne Introduction: Understanding Modern Art*. Usborne Publishing Ltd., 1991

Borja, Corinne and Robert. *Making Collages*. Albert Whitman & Co., 1972

Brown, Laura Krasny and Marc. *Visiting the Art Museum*. E.P. Dutton, 1986

Cumming, Robert. *Just Look...A Book About Paintings*. Charles Scribners Sons, 1979

Glubok, Shirley. *The Art of Colonial America*. Macmillan, 1970

Greenberg, Jan and Sandra Jordan. *The Painter's Eye*. Delacorte Press, 1991

Hurd, Thacher and John Cassidy. *Watercolor for the Artistically Undiscovered*. Klutz Press, 1992

Isaacson, Philip M. *A Short Walk Around the Pyramids and Through the World of Art*. Alfred A. Knopf, 1993

Janson, H.W. and Anthony F. Janson. *History of Art for Young People*. Henry N. Abrams, 1992

Milord, Susan. *Adventures in Art*. Williamson Publishing, 1990

Moore, Reavis. *Native Artists of North America*. John Muir Publications, 1993

Pekarik, Andrew. *Painting Behind the Scenes*. Hyperions Books for Children, 1992

Peppin, Anthea. *The Usborne Story of Painting*. Usborne Publishing Ltd., 1980

Solga, Kim. *Draw!* F&W Publications, Inc., 1991

Tofts, Hannah. *The Collage Book*. Simon and Schuster, 1990

Vasari, Giorgio. *Artists of the Renaissance*. Viking Press, 1978

Ventura, Piero. *Great Painters*. G.P. Putnam's Sons, 1984

Welton, Jude. *Eyewitness Art: Impressionism*. Dorling Kindersley, 1993

Woolf, Felicity. *Picture This*. Doubleday, 1992

_____. *Picture This Century*. Doubleday, 1992

Yenawine, Philip. *Colors*. Delacorte Press, 1991 (Other titles include *Shapes; Lines; Stories*.)

Teacher Reference

Baumgardner, Jeannette Mahan. *60 Art Projects for Children*. Clarkson Potter/Publisher, 1990, 1993

Brooks, Mona. *Drawing with Children*. Jeremy P. Tarcher, Inc., 1986

Edwards, Betty. *Drawing on the Right Side of the Brain*. G.P. Putnam, 1989

Howard, Kathleen, ed. *The Metropolitan Museum of Art Guide*. The Metropolitan Museum of Art, New York, 1983

Teacher Created Materials

Connecting Art and Literature TCM — #346

Explorers TCM — #288

Masterpiece of the Month — TCM #018